Animals As Friends

A HEAD KEEPER REMEMBERS LONDON ZOO

Jim Alldis

former Head Keeper, London Zoo

TAPLINGER PUBLISHING CO., INC.

NEW YORK

First published in the United States in 1973 by
TAPLINGER PUBLISHING CO., INC.
New York, New York

© 1973 by Jim Alldis

All rights reserved

Printed in Great Britain

No part of this publication may be reproduced or transmitted
in any form or by any means, electronic or mechanical, including
photocopy, recording, or any information storage and retrieval
system now known or to be invented, without permission in
writing from the publishers except by a reviewer who wishes to
quote brief passages in connection with a review written for
inclusion in a magazine, newspaper or broadcast.

Library of Congress Catalog Card Number: 73-5275

ISBN 0-8008-0271-3

Contents

List of Illustrations

1

New Arrival at the Zoo

As a teenager, I had ambitions to become a first-class cricketer. I did in fact have five seasons at Lord's—on the ground staff. In 1927 I accepted a job at the London Zoo to fill in until I could decide what to make of my life. My only interest in animals at that time was a fondness for farm horses and dogs.

My first job at Regent's Park, on the Works Department, was making tea and hotting up the lunch-cans for the men building the Main Gate. My kitchen was under the Mappin Terraces and I watched keepers passing to and fro carrying bass brooms, shovels and pails, obviously on their way to cleaning out the bear dens on the gantry above. Sometimes they took visitors to some mysterious spot; everyone was excited, especially the children, so I guessed this must have been a privilege and something very enjoyable.

One day my curiosity got the better of me. I took the keepers a cup of tea and then wandered along the dark, gloomy passage leading to the sleeping quarters of the bears. I climbed a short wooden stairway, turned the corner—and found myself eyeball to eyeball with a full-grown Black Canadian Bear. My feet and legs went dead. If they'd had any life at all I would have been down those stairs and across the park in nothing, flat, ending at speed my brief career at the Zoo; but I heard

9

a voice say, 'It's all right, she won't hurt you', and round the corner came the keeper.

So I met Winnie the Pooh, hostess of so many At Homes. After that I often found time to go up and see her, taking with me some tinned condensed milk, for which she sat up and begged. When she had finished the milk, she would lie on her back and rock backwards and forwards as a way of saying thank you. I suppose Winnie was the reason for my deciding right then that this was my sort of thing. I had never really thought it possible that by kindness and patient training so much joy could be brought into the life of a creature in captivity. As I got to know the keepers better, I listened to their experiences with envy, for I could see they thought the world of Winnie—as the cuss-words showed!

I asked for a transfer to the Menagerie Department, and in June 1928 I became the most junior of the staff in the sanatorium, tending the needs of a wide variety of sick or newly arrived inmates. There I met Peter, the baby elephant, no more than thirty-six inches high; Kathleen, the young black rhinoceros, and the nanny goat. These happily shared a den together and caused a sensation with young visitors when they took their exercise stroll round the Zoo. The goat would be led; Peter would follow the goat anywhere. Kathleen would butt the young elephant from behind—playfully, of course— to keep up the speed, with no lagging on the way. Peter first showed me the uncanny control even a young elephant has with its trunk. He could lift a four-pint glass bottle filled with milk and manoeuvre it so that the neck of the bottle came into his mouth, without spilling the milk or breaking the bottle. Sometimes, when he felt in the mood for fun and games, Peter would walk towards you from thirty or forty yards away, gradually increasing his pace so that by the time he reached you, you either jumped or were knocked flat. Our long-handled bass brooms were no use at all. He would just ignore the broom and come straight on until you dropped it and bolted. Then he would lift the broom high in the air as a sign of victory! All good fun but uncomfortable for the victim. One day I found myself on the receiving end once too often and, picking myself up from the floor, I grabbed a birch broom used by the gardeners to sweep the paths and made an attack of my own. Peter took one look at this new weapon and bolted for his life, screaming for mercy. Why one broom should be so different from another I never learned, but from then on just one small twig from a birch broom was enough to convince Peter that once playtime was over it was wiser to be well behaved.

About this time came my first big emergency, followed by a lesson in the folly of trying to anticipate the working of an animal's brain. I found myself alone on duty, only for thirty minutes, but things certainly happened. One of the park-keepers from nearby Regent's Park rang the gate bell and told me that, out in the Broad Walk some way from the Zoo, a crowd of people was highly amused at the antics of a large monkey at the top of a tree. Furthermore, if the monkey belonged to us, would I kindly do something about getting it back. I went along and found it was not only ours, but the most spiteful of the lot. Trying hard to give the impression that I had to deal with problems like this every day, though I had not in fact even qualified for my first uniform, I went to collect a catch net. A monkey in a den can, with luck and judgment, be netted in next to no time, but one at the top of a tree, in the open, and bad tempered at that, is something else. The children present, like their parents, absolutely refused to clear the area, although some of them could have been in danger. 'Ah well', I thought, 'these people expect something in the way of an effort, so here goes.'

My idea was to climb just a short distance up the tree—maybe to the first or second bough—holding the net, and then, having gone through the motions, return with dignity to the ground and send for help. As I started to climb, a great cheer went up from the crowd, and when I looked up I realised that the cheer was not for me. It was for the monkey, and he, in a foul temper, was coming down to meet me. I was in no position to defend myself. Of course, the people could not know the true situation and the hullabaloo was not helping matters. I felt his weight on my shoulders and said good-bye to an ear for a start. Hoping that what was to follow would not be too long drawn out, I froze for long, agonising seconds. Then it began to dawn on me that I was unharmed. Two cold hands were gripping tight about my neck, clinging to me for safety. Which of us had been more scared over the last minutes I can't think, but I honestly believe he was happier to see me than I was to see him. When we arrived at the sanatorium, I promised him all the good things in life for being so co-operative, and prepared to put him back in his cage. Just as I was doing this, he turned suddenly and bit my hand. Animals! Their only certainty is their uncertainty. This is just one of the things that makes being a zoo-keeper so interesting. The longer you stay at the job, the more you realise you will never know all the answers.

Forty years ago, a keeper's work day began at 6.30 am and went on until 8 o'clock in the evening, with two nights early at 5 o'clock and one day off per week. One Sunday off in four meant that week-ends away from the Zoo were practically unknown. Sunday became just another day, except that work consisted mainly of tidying up the houses, in order that Fellows of the Zoological Society and their friends could come in promptly at 9am and not be 'embarrassed' by such things as manure-collecting trucks running about.

A normal week-day for the menagerie staff went something like this. On arrival at your particular mess-room you changed into overalls and, where necessary, wellington boots, and set about cleaning the cages, dens and enclosures as instructed by the keeper in charge. He himself would then make a complete tour of inspection, checking for illness, and any births and deaths or other facts of interest, all of which, together with the temperature reading, were recorded on the appropriate sheet and sent to the main office.

The breakfast break at 8 o'clock was a ritual. We had a good fry-up and a read of the paper, all crammed into thirty minutes, but most enjoyable of all to me were the anecdotes of the more senior staff. Then back to finish the cleaning out, and unless there happened to be a public feeding with a set time, the latter part of the morning was spent in making up the foodstuffs and filling up water containers. In the sanatorium, specialised diets needed extra concentration. This also applied to houses containing newborn youngsters, pregnant females and such animals as chimpanzees which needed just that bit more attention.

By about 11.30am you could usually get yourself cleaned up and changed into uniform. Lunch times were a matter of general agreement between work mates; if you were not eating, you were expected to be somewhere in sight or sound of the public, to answer questions or help generally. During the summer afternoons, twenty or so keepers and helpers controlled the children's animal rides in the centre of the gardens. Elephants, camels, llamas, ponies and donkeys were employed from 2pm until 5pm. It was hard work and the elephant-loaders were known to lose quite a lot of weight in the holiday season, lifting two thousand or so children on and off the saddles of four elephants, and some of the 'children' were a bit long in the tooth. I was in charge of Jock, the big kiang, standing about fourteen hands, which is a fair size for a wild ass. Jock was a bit moody, but was used on extra busy days to help lighten the burden of Jenny, the Spanish somali, who just plodded around the flower beds hour after hour without a care in the world. Despite their efforts, the children on her back could never get Jenny to increase her pace, but Jock would step it out in double-quick time provided you gave him a loose rein and no one came up too quickly on his off side. He and I had a working agreement early on and had no trouble at all until one Easter Monday. With two children on his back and me walking alongside supporting them, Jock suddenly reared on to his hind legs to avoid a youngster who had rushed up to offer a tit-bit. The child stood mesmerised as the kiang towered above him. Still holding the two on the saddle, I quickly reached forward and pushed the child out of danger. I was still in the process of quietening Jock when I felt a blow on my ear, and turned to face an irate mother, who informed me in a loud voice what she would do to me if I pushed her child over again. Up rushed another woman who had witnessed the whole thing and was prepared to do battle on my behalf!

Most times you could enjoy a lot of fun with the visitors. I well recall the day when a woman, seemingly well educated, approached Albert White, the penguin keeper. Albert had been with penguins so long he actually walked like one, and when he came on duty after a little liquid refreshment at lunchtime, there was never a dull moment. That day the following conversation took place:

'Keeper, I have always wondered how you tell the difference between the male penguins and the females. They look so much alike to me.'

'Well, lady, it's not easy. You see, I have to go into the enclosure with a bucket of fish. When they all gather around I hold up a fish. If he takes it, it's a male, and if she takes it, it's a female.'

'Ah, I see! That *is* interesting. Thank you very much.'

And before she tripped happily away she insisted on Albert accepting a shilling for his kindness.

Faced with question after question, day after day, a sense of humour was a tremendous help and, although the Zoo was a place to be entertained by the animals, the uncaged staff often put on quite a show of their own. This sense of humour was sometimes put severely to the test; however careful a keeper might be, a crisis could arise, perhaps because of a momentary lack of concentration or because of the reaction of an animal. Visitors would say to me, 'I wouldn't have your job for all the tea in China', imagining that a high standard of bravery was called for. This was an exaggeration, of course, but although the uniformed staff quickly came to accept the slight element of danger as part of the job, this feeling was not always shared by the men in the Works Department who attended to the repair of the cages. On one occasion a carpenter arrived at the Lion House to refix a shelf inside one of the cages. Entrance could only be made at the end of the row, each cage being separated from the next by an iron slide secured by a padlock. So, if a man wanted to work in cage 4, the animals in cages 1, 2, and 3 were locked in their sleeping dens at the rear. Under the impression that it was safe to go through, the carpenter, Tom, ducked under slide 1, crossed the cage and made for slide 2. He dragged this open and crawled through, making for the next which was the last. As he slammed it back, he looked up straight into the eyes of a tiger, which seemed more than a little surprised by the intrusion. Tom's own version as to what followed was,

Page 17 The author with Rabiu, the cheetah

Page 18 (left) Mickey 'President of the Leopard Club'

(right) a leopard cub, much less assured than Mickey

'I remember pulling the slide shut. I remember something crashing against the other side. After that, nothing.' Tom, I should mention, suffered from a perman-
ently watering eye, the subject of much leg-pulling by
his mates. When he had somewhat recovered from his
ordeal, they really went to work on him. 'I bet the old
eyes watered, then, eh, Tom?' Tom's reply was to the
effect that his bowels gave him much greater cause for
alarm.

Another day, two keepers from the wolves' den, after
clocking in for work, made their way across the grounds,
unlocked the gate and went along the service passage to
the keepers' room. Pushing back the half-open door, they
almost fell over a spotted hyena curled up in front of
the grate. The noise of their arrival hardly disturbed
him; he simply looked up, sighed and went back to
sleep. Their first thought was a smart about-turn, but
being anxious not to startle the animal they moved
slowly and soon realised that they were quite welcome to
stay if they wished. Somehow, during the night, the hyena
had got out of his cage and, attracted by the warmth
from the room, had settled himself down. Not a stick
of furniture was out of place, though total destruction
might have been expected. Until then this particular
animal, a big male, had been treated with the greatest
respect. A hyena's jaws can work their way through the
shinbone of a horse; what chance would there be if
they closed on your arm or leg? The incident certainly
improved the relationship between this hyena and the
staff, and from that day on he was free to come and go
as he wished within the confines of the House. Asked

A

afterwards if they had been scared, the keepers replied, 'Well, our feet went up and down, but we didn't seem to be moving.'

One day Chi-Chi, the giant panda, for reasons best known to herself, suddenly attacked the young keeper who was sweeping out her enclosure. Whether he slipped or was knocked down was not clear, but as he lay on the ground the panda was trying to savage his leg. His shout for help was heard by another keeper whose only experience was with monkeys. He leapt over the wall, seized a broom and stood over the man, warding off the animal until further assistance arrived and Chi-Chi was forced back into her sleeping quarters. The hero was awarded the Society Medal for his efforts.

The methods used by more experienced men, when dealing with an animal attempting to get out of line, were often very amusing. One moment the offender would be preparing to charge, then it would be stopped dead in its tracks by a loud shout of, 'What the blankety-blank do you think you're doing? Get back in there,' and a crestfallen animal would slink away, overpowered by voice alone—or perhaps by the choice of words.

The keepers were a close-knit unit, accepting the fact that at some time or other a mate might have to step lively, but not at all worried by the prospect. Bravery was a word used only when a keeper went to the aid of a complete stranger, without a thought to his own safety, and in doing so lost his life. One of the most popular members of our clan did just that; the memory of such people cannot be erased.

2

The North Mammal House

In the early 1930s I was transferred to the North Mammal House where I was destined to stay, with the exception of the war years, until my retirement at the end of 1968. Right from the start I took to my new home. The construction of the House was simple but effective; a long building, separated into two halves. Outside were pens or cages containing tree stumps or shelves, where the animals could be seen by visitors; each den had a door or slide leading to the inner or sleeping quarters, along the length of which ran a service passage. This passage was out of bounds to the public and was the ideal place really to get to know your charges. The stock was varied in the extreme, although all were entitled to live in a mammal house by virtue of being warm blooded and capable of suckling their young. They included, among other interesting inmates, a couple of leopards, some gibbons, tree-climbing kangaroos, fennec foxes and lemurs. Two of the gibbons —Bumbas, the siamang, and Puck, the hoolock—were among the best known and their shrill shrieks could be heard as far away as Hampstead Heath. Bumbas would slowly inflate the pouch under her chin until it filled with air, like bagpipes, and then boom out the bass or low notes. Meanwhile Puck from the high point in the cage would scream in a high-pitched frenzy, 'Ah Who

Ah', which I believe is Gibbonese for, 'It's great to be alive'. When they were in full song, the cups and saucers in the mess room cupboard next door did a turn of their own.

To me the greatest joy of all was Nancy, the young leopard. I had always thought of the leopard as a mean and ferocious animal, never to be trusted and completely unmanageable. How wrong I was! Looking back, I can see that the cats were undoubtedly my first deep love. Nancy most likely began it all. One afternoon, when she was to be moved to another part of the house, she escaped from her den during the attempt to get her into the shifting box, and found her way to the opening between the two sections of the house. Only a 6ft railing separated her from the main road. Beyond that was Primrose Hill, where a flock of sheep was grazing about twenty yards away. It would have needed very little to send her over the top and in amongst them. My head keeper, the only other person present, weighed roughly eighteen stone and was getting close to pensionable age. Therefore the task of getting past Nancy, fetching a joint of meat from the safe and then stepping back again, dangling the meat like a carrot before a donkey, had to be done by me or not at all. Nancy, bless her, did not panic in the least. In fact, she followed me back into the service passage, entered her den and waited for the meat to be tossed in for her. With the door securely locked, I quietly sat down on the floor outside her cage and in a low voice talked to her in what I hoped was a language she could understand. She even left her meat to come across and lick the fingers I put through the bars to caress her. From that moment I was 'Cat Man'.

Sometimes the old adage 'fools rush in' can be applied to a keeper who acts first and thinks afterwards, as happened with me on a later occasion. One end of the North Mammal House had been walled up to make a completely separate unit known as the isolation ward. This was used as a means of segregation for animals suffering or likely to suffer from any contagious disease. As a precautionary measure, six young chimpanzees had been brought over from the Monkey House and put into the large central cage, and one of their own keepers came over each day to look after them. One afternoon the chimps broke out of their cage, went up through the fanlight and on to the roof. The cats in the cages underneath were trying to get at the disturbers of their peaceful slumbers and causing the wire netting to rock and shake all along the line. As I ran up, I was in time to see the chimps dispersing in all directions. Calling to one of my own staff to telephone the Monkey House, I tried to keep watch on all six escapees in case any crossed the roadway outside the Zoo. By the time help arrived one was on top of the exit turnstile ; another was perched on the top rail of the bridge, screaming its head off at a dog below ; two more were high in the surrounding trees, whilst the remainder ran from one vantage point to another. I saw chimps in my dreams that night! Such things as catch nets were useless ; the best thing was to get close and coax them to come to you. As they made their way towards us, we each grabbed one and thankfully carried them back inside. Mine was the last to go in, and it was only as the cigarettes were being lit to soothe our feelings that one of the Monkey House staff turned to me and said, 'Did you know you had Jubilee?' I knew Jubilee only by reputation; she had at some time or another bitten nearly all her own keepers and was thoroughly bad tempered. My leg was pulled, but again a lesson had been learned. In many cases of escape the animal becomes unsure away from the security of its own cage; it panics to such an extent that it loses all control and unless quickly recaptured would just run wild. Jubilee was, I am sure, so pleased to get back that she either forgot to bite or had no wish to, and on this occasion I had come off better than my earlier experience with the monkey from the sanatorium. That bitten hand was the first of only two minor injuries I received in the whole of my time at the Zoo, and the second I am certain was a pure accident.

When I first came to the North Mammal House, one of the gibbons was an exceptionally fine specimen of the white-cheeked variety, named Siki. Gibbons are best known for walking upright and for their tremendously long arms, which enable them to swing easily from tree to tree. Crossed above the head, the arms are also used as a means of balance when they break into a run. Siki spent the whole day outside, weather permitting, and shortly before the gardens closed one of us would open his door so that he could come in to feed and settle down for the night. He would swing from his lofty perch down into your arms, to be carried to his sleeping box where his supper and milk drink awaited him. One

evening I threw back the door and lifted my head to call
him; the next thing I knew I was staggering back with
blood streaming from my nose. A visitor who witnessed
the whole affair from the outside told me what had
happened. Some very young boys on their way to the
exit gate, making an unearthly din, frightened Siki so
much that he got into a panic and leapt for the safest
place he knew, at the very moment I opened the door.
We met in mid-air, so to speak, and before he could
regain control he bit at the object closest to him, which
happened to be my nose. As soon as he realised what
he had done he clung to me trying as best he knew to
say how sorry he was. I was still in a daze as he dis-
engaged one hand from behind my neck, gently touched
my bleeding nose and then clung tighter than ever,
whimpering all the while like a baby. When the noisy
group had passed I put him outside again, although he
didn't want to leave me. I waited a while, then went
through the whole drill, this time without mishap. Had
I reprimanded him maybe he would never have been
the same again, but hot temper and good keepership
never go together, and Siki and I were able to enjoy
each other's company for many days to come.

A good keeper should not show favouritism to a
particular animal; but no harm was done if a little dis-
cretion was used. Mammals, of course, have very definite feelings, none more so than the cat family. Make
too much fuss of one in full view of another and the
mood of the neglected one would change dramatically;
you would get little or no response to any advances
until you proved yourself all over again. This could be

done in many ways. An outsider looking through the keyhole or watching on closed-circuit television would have thought some type of witchcraft was being performed.

I well remember a new arrival from a circus which had closed down. Undoubtedly this animal, a bay lynx from South America, had never got used to the noise and ballyhoo in his former life and enjoyed his new quiet sleeping quarters so much that he simply curled up on a shelf and slept all day, showing no interest whatsoever in his surroundings. This was all very well for a while, but with no activity at all his condition would have quickly deteriorated, possibly with fatal results. The first attempts to awaken him produced snarls and violent shivering, a sure sign of shattered nerves. To remain in his sight for too long caused even more distress.

So, with the head keeper's permission, I used a therapy of my own. Several times a day I would walk past his cage, ignoring him completely, not even giving a glance in his direction. As the days went on I went slower and slower, so that I was in sight just that little bit longer. After a good two weeks of this I changed the routine, pausing a while in front of him, still not looking at him, slowly bending to tie a shoe-lace or using some other little delaying tactic. After a long course of this treatment, I would turn my back on him and rest my hands lightly on the wire mesh to help him to get my scent more easily. Then one day I felt his hot breath on my hands. His curiosity had got the better of him, he had left his shelf to investigate and the battle was half won. A short while later he was going into the outside yard in view of the public and getting the benefit of fresh air and sunshine—the finest medicine of all.

This took a long time and maybe I neglected a few other duties meanwhile, but even in those earlier days I knew the welfare of the animals must come first. Later on, when young newcomers to the staff came under my control, I pointed out to them that, unlike human beings who can voice their own complaints, animals can nevertheless by various signs of their own show when things are not going well, and it is up to the keeper to learn those signs and act accordingly. On occasions these strong views got me into hot water with members of the senior staff, and even some Fellows; but I would argue the case for the animal to the bitter end and would do the same all over again.

Just before the outbreak of World War II, I was promoted to the position of Keeper in Charge, North Mammal House. For about two years I had a say in the running of the House, and more important, could use the opportunity to make a close study of the subject nearest my heart. Just when everything appeared full of promise, the war came and I was called for other service. The North Mammal House was so near the main road, and the threat of bombing so close, that all the stock was removed to houses in the centre of the gardens. When I returned in 1945, many old favourites were missing; Nancy, the young leopard; Solomon and Sally, two cheetahs who, after weeks of patient preparation, had agreed to share a den and showed every

prospect of being the first to breed in captivity; Jeanne,
a beautiful young tigress; Jimmy, a lion cub, and Gipsy,
a Ceylon leopardess. Most had died in an epidemic
which had hit the Lion House, their new quarters.
My own home was a shambles. It had been used as a
pig farm, a junk yard and a storeroom; it took a gang
of workmen three months to clear and decorate it.

Then the restocking began and very soon some truly
delightful animals came under my care. My stock consisted of carnivores, flesh-eating animals, both canine
and feline. Although there were many species under
one roof, away from the public you never heard a growl
or a snarl of anger; they were friendly and happy with
their life in captivity.

3
Cat Man

It was a spectacular sight when a whole line of beautiful leopards were on show, each one in peak condition,
their glossy, golden bodies covered with darker coloured
rosettes. The old saying about the leopard changing
its spots would be more applicable to the cheetah; he is
marked with individual spots, whereas the leopard
markings are spots formed into clusters or rosettes, not
unlike an ivy-leaf in shape. After the necessary quarantine period was over and the cats had become used to
their new surroundings, they were quite ready to lean
close to the netting so that they could have their heads
and necks gently scratched by their adoring public.
The leopards included Bingo and Sandra from South
West Africa, Yimkin from Aden, and Mickey and
Elsie from Ceylon. Wonderful as they all were in a
group, each had an individual personality and a particular way of playing to the crowd. Bingo, for instance,
would stand still for the caresses until apparently tired
of it all, when he would slowly stroll back to his inside
den as though the show were over. He would then be
out of sight, and people would start turning away. Bingo
would then come flying into view again and hurl himself at the netting, causing those who had lingered
too long and too close to be shot half-way across the
walk. As Bingo once more walked back inside, I

swear he was laughing as much as the people outside.

I made a practice of having a play session with Bingo; one game consisted of running my hand down his back and holding on to his tail. So, when it became necessary to inject him against cat flu, it was just another game to him when I coaxed him up to the partly open slide connecting with the next den and held on to his tail. The veterinary surgeon, new to the job, had come to the House expecting a full-grown bundle of teeth and claws, which he would have to help catch and restrain. As it was, the injection was easily given and he was more than grateful and mightily relieved.

Nowadays there are many humane ways of sedating an animal—drugs in food, tranquillising darts and so on. To my mind the golden rule is, keep it simple. If you can get the job done without fuss and distress to the patient, you can always use the same method again if it becomes necessary. Once you make an animal really frightened, you had better try something else, for it will not be deceived a second time. When transferring an animal from one house to another, I always used to put the shifting-box into the den at least three days beforehand. Given time to sniff around, to enter the box and walk out again, even to urinate and mark it for possession, it would be less likely to panic when moving day arrived.

Sandra was, next to Yimkin, the smallest leopard, lighter in colouring, and so dainty and petite, so completely feminine. She had her own way of pleasing her fans. In her outside den was a good thick bough of a tree, with a forked section resting against the angle of the side wall and the roof, which made an ideal place for her to lie and sunbathe. Much as she loved this particular spot, she would always come down when she recognised someone she knew in the crowd. As she received the tickles behind her ear and other fond endearments, she would voice her pleasure with gurgling, guttural rumblings in the throat and her eyelids would droop in sheer ecstasy. When it was time for her friend to move on, Sandra would return to her perch in the tree with one graceful leap of effortless ease. It seems almost impossible for cats to make an ugly or undignified movement, and I would say the leopard in motion is the most beautiful sight of all.

Another of Sandra's little ploys was to lie in the doorway to the inner den, her body hidden except for just one eye which was focused on the front of her cage. She had recognised the voice of one of her admirers and was playing her own version of hide-and-seek. When the friend came into view, he would enter into the spirit of the game and exclaim in a loud voice, 'Well, Sandra must have moved, I'd better look somewhere else', then walk quietly away. A minute later he would return, unobserved as he thought, but waiting for him was Sandra with an 'I caught you again, didn't I?' expression on her face.

Little Yimkin too was a real treasure, lovable in nature, beautiful in appearance. 'Yimkin' I understood to be Arabic for 'perhaps, or perhaps not', and she was well named. Without a doubt, she was Pat's girl. He was the junior member of the staff in the House, and right from the start he fell for 'Yimmie' and she for

Cat Man

him; it was almost an embarrassment for the rest of us to try and get any reaction from her when Pat was around. People who were allowed the privilege of coming into the service passage at the rear of the House often asked to see her, and we would softly call to her to come forward to be petted. If Pat happened to be out of the building at the time, she would respond without hesitation; but if he was anywhere close at hand she just looked right through whoever it was and lay contented on her bed of straw. Then, of course, Pat was asked to demonstrate. Yimkin would come to his call without a glance at anyone else, and roll on her back or turn somersaults, all the time purring with pleasure at the sound of her master's voice. A favoured few of the Fellows could also rely on a warm welcome from Yimkin, but for myself it was 'perhaps, perhaps not'; although she lost nothing in the way of my affection for her.

Cats have minds of their own and should be respected for it; my love for them and theirs for me was something beyond value. About this time I was an officer of the Staff Association, either chairman or secretary, and as with any other organisation there were problems which at times seemed insurmountable. After a particularly difficult meeting, I always found the finest relaxation was to walk along and have a social session with my cats. There was nothing to compare with it.

Elsie and Mickey completed the leopard display, and display it certainly was. Elsie lacked nothing in appearance or temperament and was full entertainment value, but the whole bunch was ruled by Mickey, the President of the Leopard Club. A very old friend, James Dyrenforth, well known in the world of show business, had been a regular visitor to the House since pre-war days and it was he who formed the club. Membership was confined to a limited group of real cat-lovers; people whose genuine interest and correct behaviour were a real influence in making their favourites contented. I say 'correct behaviour' because on occasion a particularly loud-voiced individual, showing off in front of his friends, might unsettle the animals. Needless to say, he was never invited again. Mickey, as president, had his own visitors' book, with many famous names in it: Sir Malcolm Sargent, Constant Lambert, Ronnie Waldman, Frank Muir, Harry Pepper, Martin Boddey, and Dame Laura Knight, who sketched an entry in the book as a Christmas card for him.

Mickey's affection for me was touching and, during the summer months when the Public Walk was full of people, he would stand on his hind legs to peer over their heads to watch me go out of sight as I left the Zoo on my evenings off. Even when I was out of uniform, he recognised me in a crowd without any effort on my part. Apart from the keepers, his favourite was Jimmy Dyrenforth. Between them was a mutual regard, almost an affinity, which I respected. I did not intrude when they were together, for Jimmy's visits were necessarily limited to Wednesdays and Sundays. After the neck rubbing and behind-the-ears tickle had been completed to his satisfaction, Mickey would reach up to lick the side of Jimmy's face and I know from my own experience the agony that would follow next day when Jimmy attempted to shave. A leopard's tongue feels like sandpaper, but the discomfort can be easily endured when you remember the honour bestowed upon you.

This bond between man and animal cannot be easily explained away nor can anyone not having experienced such a relationship understand the depth to which such feeling can go. When Jimmy Dyrenforth was forced to return to the States for family reasons, and expected to be away for six months or so, he admitted to me that he dreaded the thought of Mickey forgetting him during his long absence. After he left, although Mickey remained exactly the same on five days during the week, somehow it appeared that on Wednesdays and Sundays something was missing. He still had plenty of friends keen to fill the gap, but there was just that little difference.

Then one day, long afterwards, I was standing at the entrance to the House, with my shoulder resting against the wire of Mickey's outdoor cage. He had been fast asleep on his wooden shelf for some time. Suddenly, he became wide awake and, not even waiting to stretch (which is the most natural thing for a cat to do), he jumped down, came bounding across to the corner where I stood, becoming more and more excited, and finally climbing half-way up the netting to get a clear view down towards the North Gate. Within a couple of minutes Jimmy Dyrenforth came into sight and Mickey disappeared to his inner quarters, waiting eagerly for his friend. Coincidence? Strong sense of

Page 35 Willing volunteers were always happy to assist with young animals, particularly those neglected by their mothers; (*above*) a lion cub being coaxed to finish his vitamin-seasoned food; (*below*) lion cub Keno receiving a little help at feeding time

Page 36 (left) A young cheetah looks apprehensive on arrival at the Zoo

(right) Rabiu, a happily established adult cheetah, shows his affection for his keeper

smell? Some curious mystic power? I still don't know. Jimmy came up to me. 'Do you think he will remember me?' he asked. I just smiled and said, 'Go in and see for yourself.' I entered the passageway some time later and there they were, alone in their own little world.

When Jimmy heard in 1949, through the Zoo bush telegraph, that Whipsnade Zoo wanted a leopard, he immediately adopted Mickey, paying ten shillings a week towards his upkeep on the understanding that he remained in London.

Tishy, the golden cat from Assam, resembled a miniature puma with rather long legs. He had a glorious coat like burnished gold, a long tail lined pure white, and facial markings completely unlike those of any other cat large or small. I have never before or since seen anything to compare with Tishy's lightning reflexes. The co-ordination of mind, eye and muscle were something you had to see to believe. In his indoor cage where he was fed last thing at night, there stood a forked tree in the farthermost corner about 14ft from the gate. His favourite dish was a dead rabbit with the fur left on, but instead of starting his meal at once, Tishy always spent fifteen minutes or so playing to the gallery. He would pick up the carcass in his mouth, carry it over to the front of the cage, retreat half-way back leaving the rabbit there at your feet and invite you to try and touch it through the netting. As soon as you bent down he would spring forward and whip it away, throwing it to all corners of the cage as he sped around after it. This game went on until he began to tire; then came the

B

amazing feat which he always saved for the grand finale. Grabbing the rabbit in his mouth he would run up the tree, turn to face his audience and hurl the rabbit the whole width of his cage; he would be down from the tree and across the floor in time to catch it before it hit the ground. Then, and not before, he would begin to eat it. Even knowing what to expect, it was difficult to follow his speed of movement, and although I must have watched him a hundred times, I never saw him miss his catch. Tishy was yet another extremely friendly cat, well behaved to everyone, exceptionally so to the select few he looked upon as his special humans. To greet these favoured ones he would stand in the doorway between his inner and outer quarters and utter what I supposed to be a miaow, which started as a throat gargle and ended with a call like a Siamese cat.

The cat with the most striking markings was Peter, the clouded leopard from the East Indies. His coat was like that of a python as far as the pattern was concerned, the shapes outlined in black over a body of yellowy brown. The whole effect was more reptilian than feline, but none the less beautiful. Peter was shyer than most, coming forward only to those people he knew really well. Those who did not belong to his inner circle could only admire from a distance, for he never believed in exerting himself and was always the last one to get up in the morning. During the summer months he would simply walk to the outer den, pick a corner where the sun shone to the best advantage and curl up until mid-day. The House faced south and the sun was the finest tonic of all to keep the cats in good condition.

One animal above all others loved the warm summer days; this was Caesar, a leopard who had come to us from a privately owned zoo about to close down. Poor Caesar had lived in an enclosure completely exposed to all weathers, with not even a bed of straw or a covered shed to retire to at night, and because of this callous treatment he had a bad rheumatic condition. From the day he came to us we were determined the last years of his life were going to be a great deal happier. A big pile of wood wool shavings made a snug warm bed, where he could stretch out in comfort. His greatest difficulty was freedom of movement after a night of deep sleep, and to watch him dragging himself around for the first hour or two was sickening. This stiffness, with the help of the warm sun, gradually wore off and Caesar was able to enjoy the rest of the day free from pain. An infra-red lamp was a permanent fixture above his bed and helped when the weather was not so kind. He never fully recovered, but the general improvement was remarkable and as time went on he gathered his own group of admirers around him.

'Keeper, your cheetah must be ill, he has been crying!' Many times I have answered the gate bell of the North Mammal House to hear this from a small, solemn-faced child. The cheetah's head is marked by lines running from each side of his nose down to the corners of his mouth, for all the world like tear stains. In 1960 the London Zoo received a magnificent young cheetah, one of two found abandoned in Nigeria. He was the first I had known from West Africa and quite different in appearance from any others. Rabiu, meaning 'African chief', was longer-legged, very much lighter in colouring and more of a greyhound type as compared with the stocky or bulldog build of Abdul, another male already in residence. The first few months following Rabiu's 'capture', if the picking up of a bundle of fur could be so described, were spent in the bungalow home of an ex-patriate. When he got too big and frolicsome for comfort, and children were bowled over as he amiably joined them at play, he came to us. After the necessary quarantine period, he was slowly taught to accept a collar and lead. His temperament was a strange mixture of fondness for myself and a tendency to go completely haywire when you least expected it. His sheer high spirits were good to see, for it was a sure sign of excellent health; but his was far and away the most untidy den in the House, with bedding scattered everywhere as he dashed around playing his puppy games. When at last he settled down enough, I started him on his outside walks, only to find that he had still one trick up his sleeve. We would be striding out in good style going quite fast, and he would suddenly decide it was time to rest; so, without any warning at all, he would halt in mid-stride, cross one of his legs over mine and hold it so that I had to stop. He would then calmly sit down and refuse to budge until he was ready. Try moving a cheetah on when he wants to stop and you will find the stubborn mule has a serious rival.

Whilst in motion the cheetah is a loose-limbed example of perfect co-ordination, muscles rippling with each step he takes, but when he wants to sit down, the contrast is quite amazing. From his head right down to his hindquarters he goes absolutely rigid and this fixity will remain in spite of all the pulling, pushing or coaxing you might try. This refusal to move until ready might well be one of the reasons why a cheetah is not used in a circus ring. In my personal opinion, there is no such thing as a 'tame' cheetah, in the truest sense of the word, though a 'trained' cheetah is another matter. Because of their extremely gentle nature and their liking for the human race, you get cheetahs to adapt themselves for training, but I found the trick was to concentrate on things they would do naturally and turn this to your advantage. Though generally accepted as the fastest thing on four legs, being capable of a speed approaching 70 mph over 400 yards, cheetahs are about the laziest of all cats, only really exerting themselves when the occasion demands it.

It was thus quite a simple matter to get Rabiu to sit down, as he was always ready to do so from choice; you merely gave the command and at the same time pressed lightly with your hand on the hindquarters. Sound of voice alone would have no effect whatsoever, but the helping hand was gratefully accepted, and saved him the trouble of learning the meaning of words, a task well beyond the powers of a cheetah's brain. When I entered Rabiu's outside den, the viewing public were thrilled to watch him jump to the top of a tree stump as I snapped my fingers and said 'Up'. This was not complete obedience on his part, merely the fact that once he was comfortably seated on the top of the stump

he was given a drink of milk from a bowl, and like all
felines much preferred to be above ground level when
stationary. Rabiu became a great favourite, though I
was careful always to put his lead on when children
accompanied their parents into the cage. He no doubt
still retained memories of his early upbringing in
Nigeria, when he was allowed to romp and play with
his former owner's little boy. On the lead, however, he
stood or sat quite confidently whilst the youngsters
stroked his head and fondled his ears. Rabiu remained
a good-tempered animal all his life, always reliable
and of mild disposition, though he would not allow
anyone to take liberties with him.

A cheetah can equally be described as a dog-like cat
or a cat-like dog. The small head with rough surfaced
tongue is true cat, but the hindquarters and non-retract-
able claws are dog family. For the first six months or so
there is some movement possible in the claws, enough
to allow moderate success in tree climbing, but they soon
become fixed and blunt like the dog's. The exception is
the dew claw, carried high on the wrist; this is the one
to watch out for and is the cheetah's main weapon of
attack. A lightning swift slash with this two-inch-long,
curved and needle-pointed claw could open up a man's
arm or leg from one end to the other. Because of this,
I would never bend over to rub a cheetah's tummy
when it was rolling on its back. Striking out with no
malice at all, just from the enjoyment of the game, he
could cause the loss of an eye to his playmate.

At the time when Rabiu was about six years old,
Abdul was the only other cheetah at the Zoo. In 1960,

Krefeld Zoo in Germany had reported the first births
of cheetahs in captivity and Rome Zoo continued the
good work a couple of years later, but it was obvious
that this animal was becoming more and more scarce.
No longer was he sighted in India, and the African
variety was dwindling. Extra effort on the part of several zoos was made to find and marry up a good breeding pair to try and preserve what had become one of
the most popular exhibits. Total extinction in the wild
during the next twenty years is possible, and it is a real
pleasure to write of a great breeding success at Whipsnade Park Zoo in Bedfordshire, where Juanita has so
far produced three litters and may well add to this
proud record. I look back and think what might have
been with our cheetahs, Sally and Solomon, had not the
war come to upset all our careful preparations. In a
belated effort to try all over again, I was sent to Bremen
in West Germany to vet and bring back two females,
afterwards named Cherry and Melanie, but to my deep
regret the suitable opportunity to arrange a pairing did
not arise before my retirement. Being denied the sight
of newly born cheetah cubs must rank as my one big
disappointment in a long career.

Many other cats graced the North Mammal House
with their particular beauty at one time or another.
From various regions of South America came the ocelot,
with the glorious silken sheen glowing over the splen-
didly-marked, leopard-like body, and the much smaller,
but equally striking, margay; the Geoffroys Cat; the
long-haired Pampas Cat, very Persian in appearance;
and the ill-named Jaguarondi, which is more like a

member of the otter family than a cat. Asian residents were represented by the snow leopard, its almost white body covered with blackish, irregular and not completely rosetted markings, and a long curling tail, as long again as the rest of the body; the Pallas Cat, very long haired and Persian looking, but its extra wide forehead and vicious temper ruled out any possibility of confusion with the Pampas Cat; and the Indian Leopard Cat, small but extremely quick in movement and a delight to watch. The long-legged serval and the tassel-eared caracal lynx came to us from the sandy terrain of West Africa.

Yes, cats I have certainly seen aplenty, from the largest to the smallest. The impression that will stay with me for ever is the dignity and grace that is theirs alone.

Page 45 Gigi, a caracal lynx presented to the Zoo by King Hussein of Jordan, with her ten-week-old kitten whose ears already show the first sign of tufts

Page 46 (*left*) Gigi's kitten at an even younger stage

(*right*) The debut at two weeks old of Butch and Ben, born to the pumas, Lola and Sabre

Page 47 The magnificent head of Sabre, the puma

Page 48 (above) Prince, the cheetah, accepting ice cream from the author's daughter, Barbara
(right) Ava Gardner with Prince after their appearance in the film *Mogambo*

4
Special Friends

SABRE

Sabre was a puma. This cat is also known as mountain lion, catamount, cougar, painter or panther. Its habitat extends from Canada right down the west coast of America to the Argentine and beyond. The largest type, found nearest to the Rocky Mountains, are called cougars; the smallest, in the extreme south, are pumas. For more reasons than one, Sabre should have been labelled 'cougar'. He was born at the foot of the Rockies and taken, while still a baby, to a Royal Canadian Air Force base, the home of the Cougar Squadron and their Sabre jets. For about five months, the camp cook coped as best he could with the little bundle of fury; most puma cubs are savage little devils and Sabre was no exception. When he came to the North Mammal House, the change in no way improved his temper, and he spat and snarled at all who dared go near him. His body weight on arrival was 30 to 35lb; towards the end of his long life he was tipping the scale at 180lb. He was the largest and best of his kind I have ever seen, a 'cougar' without a doubt. His temper took a long time to mellow. Once he sprang at the wire in an attempt to reach a keeper who was trying to soothe away some of the fear which I am sure was the root of the trouble, but missed

his footing on the edge of his shelf and fell to the ground.
As a result, he sprained a shoulder and from this
developed a slight limp. This he could turn on and off
at will, and as a means of inviting sympathy it stood
him in very good stead. One minute he would be pacing
around the den without a care in the world, but if he
saw you watching him he would go into a slower, lab-
oured walk until you moved on. Of course, there were
times, such as prolonged periods of rain or extreme
cold, when Sabre suffered from creaking joints and
most likely a spot of arthritis had set into his old injury,
but as he became older and wiser he made the most of
his disability.

Growing into maturity, he gradually lost his fear of
man and became one of the most popular animals in the
House, both with staff and visitors. I quickly learned
that, if I placed my hand on the wire mesh, he
would rub against it to enjoy the feeling of a caress;
but, if I put my fingers through the mesh for direct
contact, he would draw away in protest at such indig-
nity. If I had previously been stroking one of the other
pets, he would get the strange scent and stay well back
until I went and washed my hands; then he would
come forward at once to be extra affectionate, as if to
say, 'Why bother with them when I am here?'

Sabre had his own special friend, the wife of one of
the Fellows. She was a great help to us when the big
puma was in the process of changing coat. The cheetahs
could be groomed by brush and comb; the leopards
rolled in their bedding to get rid of any loose fur, but
Sabre, who preferred to sleep on a wooden platform,

would have been a problem without this lady's help.
Twice a week she would come to the Zoo, sit on a stool
outside his den and patiently pull out all the old matted
hair whilst Sabre, knowing it was for his own good, stood
perfectly still, drooling with pleasure.

The 'Saga of Sabre' began one day when I noticed
a small wound on his flank. The mystery of how he
came by it was never solved, though the hole in the
centre of the sore area could have been caused by a
pellet from an air gun. To try and relieve the pain,
Sabre had already licked the trouble spot until it was
quite raw; and all attempts to get ointment or a heel-
ing spray treatment on the wound failed because it was
licked off as fast as you got it on. The constant licking
with the rasp-like tongue caused the hole to become
deeper and ulcerated so that it was necessary to transfer
the patient into hospital. Before the operation to cut
out the affected area could be performed, Sabre had to
be put to sleep. It was whilst he was under the anaesthetic
that his heart stopped beating and for long agonising
seconds he was apparently dead. Some first-class veterinary work dragged him back from the brink and the
operation was quickly completed. I could not be present
whilst all this was going on, for the Zoo hospital, which
must be the finest of its kind in the world, has the stric-
test rules applying when the operation theatre is in use,
but when I next met the veterinary officer I shook his
hand in gratitude.

The following morning we brought Sabre home.
With one side of him completely shaven, the stitches
inserted to draw the flesh together again were plainly

visible and poor Sabre looked a sorry object for a week
or so. Then, as his strength began to return, once again
he began to lick his side and our worries started all over
again. I put one of the staff constantly on watch and,
as Sabre's tongue went to work, a weak solution of
warm, soapy water was squirted into his face from a
garden syringe as a reminder not to do it. This was
very effective during working and daylight hours, but
we could tell he had been up to his tricks again during
the night. I had already been warned that because of his
age he could not survive another operation and I was in
despair as I sought an answer to the problem. Because
he was such a giant compared with the females of his
kind at the Zoo, it was never considered advisable to
mate him. Now I resolved to risk everything and from
the other end of the House I brought Lola, a nice,
youngish puma, and put her into Sabre's den. There is
always a certain amount of risk in pairing pumas, even
when the female is in season and ready for mating. To
do it out of season was asking for trouble, but once over
his astonishment at the sight of his attractive visitor,
Sabre began to shower attention on her, following her
around all day long and in his excitement not bothering
to lick his sore place. As the wound healed and his fur
began to grow again, the courtship blossomed, until one
day the marriage was finally sealed and some ninety
days later Sabre became the proud father of twins,
Butch and Ben. The vet told me it was the finest
example of occupational therapy he had ever known.
Married life certainly agreed with the old rascal, and
he and Lola set up house together as though it was the

most natural thing in the world. The following year the
union was blessed with another happy event, this time
there was only one cub, but what a cub. Twice the
average size at birth, Kanook was without doubt a
chip off the old block. He grew faster than any other
cub I have known, and before he was one year old he
weighed over 100lb of solid bone and muscle, looking
more and more like his father every day. When Sabre
passed on at the ripe old puma age of sixteen, it helped
to soften the blow to know he had left behind a son
almost a replica of himself.

COOCHIE

Walk around any zoo in the world and if you can find a
more attractive animal than a little fennec fox from
North Africa I shall be very surprised. Coochie was
delightful. Her luxurious, light golden fur was designed
to make her invisible against the desert sands; her
magnificent brush or tail of slightly darker hue would
make the ideal wrap to pull over her head when she was
curled up to sleep, and the toes on her tiny feet had a
special protection against sand clogging. Her big dark
brown eyes in the little, sharp pointed face were especially appealing. But her greatest feature was her
extraordinary long ears, which were flicked, cocked or
lowered to register any different emotion and, when
extended sideways to their extreme length, looked like
the wings of an aircraft. Living on sand and spending
a lot of time in shallow burrows, the fennec fox needs
super-sensitive hearing to alert it to food (birds alight-

ing; locusts or other insects on the move nearby) and to danger, and its ears are almost like radar. Coochie weighed about 4lb and was the spoiled baby of the house. I cannot remember a single person who was not captivated by her special form of beauty. Although it took long months of patient training for her to conquer her natural shyness and reserve, she too became a star in her own right. She was always included in the Zoo's television series and I remember one shot of her when the whole screen was filled with her pretty little face and long ears.

Coochie was the first of her kind to arrive since 1934 and, according to the records and the confirmation of long-service keepers, two to three years was the average time fennecs had existed in captivity, at least in London. It is a great pleasure to record that Coochie lived a full and thoroughly happy life for all of ten years, and apart from one or two days when she was not quite her usual self, her health never gave us any cause for concern.

Strangely enough she had been with us for about five years before we heard her make any sound at all. Our good friend the Fellow's wife, who loved Sabre so much, also had a very deep attachment for Coochie. After visiting her puma friend, who was the largest and heaviest of our charges, she would then sit with little Coochie, the smallest of our family, and feed her with shelled peanuts from a paper bag. One day she arrived without first shelling the nuts and began to do it just before she made her way into the cage. Hearing the rustle of the paper bag and popping of nuts must have

been too much for Coochie, who dashed up and down
uttering a shrill chatter of excitement, and at last proved
to everyone she certainly had a tongue. From that day
on, her special friend was greeted with noisy rapture,
and the din did not subside until she was settled on the
lady's lap and taking the nuts from her fingers. As a
pick-pocket Coochie would have held her own with the
best; her little nose would move into any pocket containing an item of interest and the first you knew of the
theft was when you saw her busily trying to bury her
spoils in the deep box of sand in the corner.

PRINCE

During the restocking period after the war two cheetahs
arrived from Kenya. They were brother and sister from
the same litter, five and a half years old, called Perry and
Jenny. As they had always been together, they shared
the same den. It was obvious from the beginning that
Jenny was not too robust and needed that much more
careful observation and attention. She was a friendly
creature and loved to be petted, but first you had to push
her brother out of the way, for it seemed his main object in life was to protect her. Just how much affection
was felt between them became known to us all when,
after a short illness, Jenny contracted pneumonia and
died. The loss of his sister affected Perry so much that
he immediately went off his feed and shunned all efforts
to console him. This was doubly serious, for once a
cheetah becomes unwell it can deteriorate and lose
condition at an alarming rate. After consulting the vet,

I pleaded for Perry to remain under my care, rather than submit him to the boxing up and transfer into hospital where he would be deprived of his known keepers. For long hours every day I sat on the straw bed alongside Perry, stroking him and petting him, occasionally offering tender morsels of offal for him to swallow. To keep his mouth moist I would dip my fingers in milk and rub them over his tongue. Just when I had begun to despair, he responded by feeding from the palm of my hand, ever so little at a time, but a start at least. When at last he began to eat in bulk, and drink egg and milk from his bowl, I knew he would get well, for now the medicines he needed as a supplement could be given in his food.

Perry's recovery began a new chapter in my career. As he regained his strength, he grew in looks too; to see him becoming once again the beautiful sleek and gloriously marked creature, softly purring with pleasure at every opportunity, was reward enough. But what was to follow was a revelation. All the affection he had formerly shown his sister was now given to me, and the next nine years must go down on record as the happiest period of my life. As we watched his stately, dignified walk around his den we felt as if we were in the presence of something almost regal. So it was that I decided to change his name to Prince.

He was a magnificent animal, with a golden body covered in dark brown spots, and a most beautiful tail $3\frac{1}{2}$ft long, almost white and black-ringed all the way down to the tip. When he looked at you with his large brown eyes, he drew you as though by a magnet. His

Page 57 (*left*) Young Himalayan wolf with volunteer helper; (*right*) a pair of six-week-old European wolf cubs born to Sumie; they were the first of their kind to be born at the Zoo for twenty years and make an interesting comparison with the Himalayan type

Page 58 (*above*) Chappie, the three-year-old husky, stretches out a gentle and friendly paw; (*below*) a pair of Mexican hairless dogs, housed at the Zoo during the compulsory quarantine period; the lack of a covering coat could cause problems in the cold weather and wheat-germ oil was necessary in their diet

expression was so soft and completely relaxed, and his gentle nature had a marked effect on many of his visitors. I have seen two hard-headed businessmen finally agree on a contract after a session in his den—I even supplied the pen to sign the paper. One day I caught three young boys poking sticks through the wire and stabbing animals to provoke them into reaction. I grabbed the eldest boy, a lad of about twelve, and bundled him inside the Mammal House, where he no doubt expected what he thoroughly deserved, a hiding. Instead, I dragged him into Prince's cage with me, ignoring his terrified pleas. When he was quiet, I coaxed him into stroking Prince, though he almost passed out with fright. I explained that most of the animals they had been tormenting wanted to be friendly, and here was one that was the friendliest of all. To his credit, the kid did say he was very sorry, and when he rejoined his mates outside I saw him take away their sticks and break them in half before throwing them away. I have an idea the lesson he was given had a more lasting effect than the clip round the ear he was used to getting.

Prince was far and away the brainiest of all the cheetahs I have known and I would nominate him as the nearest to being tame. His appearances on television and in films made him famous. The extraordinary way in which he would carry out a scene gave the impression that he had received specialised training, but everything was strictly impromptu; he did just as he pleased in his own time. Any attempt to hurry him, however, would have resulted in panic. During the filming of

C

Mogambo at MGM Studios, Boreham Wood, I
watched Prince share the limelight with Ava Gardner in
two important scenes. He played his part so well and
with so little fuss that John Ford, the director, said he
wished some of his human actors were half as good. It
was a revelation to watch Prince strolling round, mixing
with the cast and the camera crew. He was in his element, with all his majesty and perfect manners, doing
everything just right. But for another film, this time
for television, he was required to snarl. This behaviour
was unknown to him and background noises were sub-
stituted to good effect. In one tricky drawing-room
scene, I was playing a blinded German baron, and
could not watch what Prince might be doing; but he
searched for my hand and sat licking it as the cameras
rolled, just as the shot demanded.

Prince preferred to travel to his engagements in an
open trailer which allowed him plenty of light and air,
although we always covered the top with a strong twine
netting to ensure safety. As there was only room for
one passenger in the cab of the lorry which pulled it,
my young colleague, Pat, sometimes travelled in the
trailer with Prince. One day, after a function at Battersea Park, where Prince's performance had gone without
a hitch, we allowed him his usual few minutes to receive
the plaudits of his admiring audience. He calmly sat on
the top of the pavilion steps gazing at the crowd just
below whilst the photographers made the most of their
opportunity. A path was cleared so that the trailer could
be brought up closer, then at the word of command,
Prince leapt into it and I began to fasten the netting,

leaving one corner for Pat to climb through. As I turned and said, 'In you go, son', a woman with umbrella raised charged through the crowd screaming, 'You cruel beast, you! Fancy making a young lad go in with a wild animal', and she aimed a blow at my head. As I dodged away, both Pat and I tried to calm her fears, but she was still not satisfied. As we drove off, the last I heard was 'I'll report you to the RSPCA'.

In the early days of television at Alexandra Palace, animals had to be carried in their boxes up a narrow spiral staircase to the studio on the top floor, but by the time Prince was ready to enjoy his first showing, TV cameramen were coming to the Zoo to make use of the specially prepared sets. So it was a simple job to lead him over to the Main Gardens to be filmed and come back home in no time at all. I never knew a cheetah who liked leaving a well-lighted area to enter one of complete darkness, and Prince was no exception. Once, after an evening show, we were on our way back when we came to the tunnel leading to the North Gardens and found nothing but inky blackness, as the lights had fused. Prince simply stopped, sat down and refused to move. It was quite some time before one of our lorries came by, and the driver was good enough to switch on the headlights to light up the tunnel and then follow us all the way home in case we came across any more dark patches. This driver came to know Prince very well, for he always volunteered to take us on our many trips outside the zoo, to various film studios, to Battersea Park or the Odney Club by the Thames at Cookham, not to mention the cinema in Paddington where Prince once took part in a 'parade of gladiators' to publicise the film *Quo Vadis*.

Providing I was present, he would allow anybody to enter his cage at the North Mammal House, although if we had allowed *all* his friends this privilege there would have been no time to complete the rest of the day's chores. When it became known that vanilla ice-cream was his top favourite tit-bit, quite a few of his friends brought some along, and Prince would run to greet his visitors, impatiently nuzzling the hand whilst the wrapper was being removed. But this kindness had to be strictly vetted for health reasons: cheetahs, like children, suffer from tummy-aches.

One young girl, Jill by name, was brought by her father to see Prince every time she had a holiday from school. After the first introduction, she received a welcome with a routine all her own. Prince would remain perfectly still on his straw bed until a stool had been placed in position. Jill, comfortably seated, would then call him and he would advance to sit at her side, licking first her hands then her face, purring with pleasure as his little friend fondled him. Some inner sense seemed to advise him that a too boisterous approach could cause distress, and his behaviour was exemplary; for Jill was completely blind.

5
Dogs from the Wild

When I first arrived at the North Mammal House, a thylacine wolf was in residence, the only one of its kind known to be in captivity. A curious animal with a mean nature, it had a long, lean body of darkish mustard colour, striped with black bars across the hindquarters, and a narrow head with long and tremendously powerful jaws which it was always ready to use. He died about 1932 and, as I was alone in the House at the time and have never since heard of one being sighted even in his native land of Tasmania, I can claim to be the last person to have seen a thylacine wolf alive.

In terms of zoological value, we had some of the finest specimens of the dog world in our care at one time or another. There was Sumie, the European wolf, who had her own little band of admirers and was always ready to lick their fingers; Changi, the Himalayan wolf; Twinky, the bush dog; Tonga, the highly strung hyena; and Chappie, a lovable husky, and his mate, Meg.

Tonga, a female hyena, was extremely good, drooling at the mouth and uttering strange little grunts of pleasure as fingers were poked through the netting to stroke her. Never once did she attempt to bite. One person above all others she was always pleased to see was a Fellow of the Zoological Society who for years made a practice of a regular Sunday morning visit. One wet day he came to the house and as usual hurriedly made his way down the passage to see his favourite, unbuttoning his raincoat as he did so. Tongo was half-way across her den ready to greet him when he absentmindedly shook his coat to get rid of the raindrops. Her hackles, or mane, shot straight up, her eyes turned blood red, and she stood for a moment or so stiff with fright. Then with a roar of anger she turned and bolted through the door leading to her outside yard. From that day she would not tolerate her former friend at any price, although remaining well behaved with everyone else. Many times afterwards he told me he would give anything to be able to win forgiveness for his mistake, but Tonga's attitude remained unaltered, and he stayed away to avoid distressing her more.

Chappie had been brought back by an expedition from North Greenland, where he was born and had worked as a sledge-dog. When he arrived at the Zoo, I had to collect him from his former owners at the Society's main office and lead him through the crowds all the way to the North Bank. Although still young, Chappie was a huge dog, dark red and cream in colouring and most fearsome in appearance. I was not at all sure how he would take to me, and was mightily relieved when we reached our destination without incident. As soon as he had become firmly settled, he was allowed to run free in the area around the House, but always before the official opening time for visitors and with one of our staff to watch him. He very soon found his way to the canal bridge, connecting the North and Middle Gardens on our side with Prince Albert Road and the outer circle of Regent's Park. Here Chappie would wait until some unsuspecting nanny or mother taking her child into the park came across the bridge. Of course, they stopped to admire the beautiful dog sitting so quietly on the other side of the railings. Chappie would allow both adult and child to stroke him, and then, once they were close enough, he would grab the doll, or whatever the child might be carrying, and bolt back to his den and bury the prize under his straw bed. Never once did he chew up or destroy any of his treasures, and when they were returned to their owners tears were soon dried, with no hard feelings. Chappie on the bridge was a sight eagerly awaited each morning by lots of young children, but they learned to keep their toys out of reach.

One day a woman caught sight of him from the top deck of a No 74 bus passing along the main road. She told the rest of the passengers about the wolf she had seen. By the time the bus reached Baker Street, it was a pair of wolves that had been sighted, and, by Knightsbridge, a whole pack running free. Telephone calls began coming in from the police; squad cars were appearing from everywhere, and I was getting more and more fed up, assuring everyone that my four wolves *were* all securely locked up and always had been. When the mystery was solved, it was decided to put a short news item in the daily papers telling people of Chappie's morning romps and asking them not to confuse him with a wolf. More than once his resemblance to a wolf came in useful when I had to deal with groups of teenagers out to make mischief. If I asked them to behave and it had no effect, I went inside and put a lead on Chappie's collar and led him out. Now, I say 'led', but as a matter of fact he loathed a lead and pulled hard to get free, dragging me with him. Promises of reformation among the teenagers soon followed.

Among the ugliest inhabitants at the House were the pouched marsupials known as Tasmanian Devils. This animal resembles a very large rodent, its body black and rotund, with short legs seeming to shoot out sideways, a large head and very powerful jaws. The short, almost upright ears when seen against the light are almost transparent. He is a devil in both looks and temper. It was said that a small group of them would kill or maim the best part of a flock of sheep in one night, so I can well imagine that the Tasmanian sheep farmers used every means of ridding the country of them, as well as their partner in crime, the thylacine wolf. I was told by an Australian that the Devils, having sighted a grazing ground, would dig themselves a long shallow trench directly confronting the approaching flock, preferably at dusk. Lying on their backs, jaws open and ready, they waited for the sheep, head to ground as they cropped the grass, to come within striking distance, then snap, the throat was severed and the killer would move along the trench to await the next victim. This would go on until they grew tired of what to them was an enjoyable pastime; then they would gorge themselves from the small neck bones, which were their particular fancy, and roll over too full to move.

This was the time when they themselves were most vulnerable and the farmers dealt out a swift vengeance as dawn disclosed the havoc that had been done. The many carcases provided rich fare for the wolf, never far away from his blood-thirsty friends.

The extraordinary maned wolf of South America was another of our residents. It differs in every way from its European, Canadian or Asian cousins, which though varying a little in size can generally be recognised as wolves. The maned wolf is fox-like in its reddish-brown colouring, with a medium-length brush, white underneath and black tipped, a very narrow chest and body, and a long-jawed, rather attractive head. It is best described by the names given to it by the tribesmen in its native land—'Fox on Stilts' or 'Ghost Wolf'. It has a very swift walking pace on long, spindly legs performed with a gaited action, that is to say, the front and the back legs on the same side rose and fell simultaneously. A 'fox on stilts, is a fair enough description. The lengthy mane and the whole body-covering consisted of hair of a delicate texture so fine that the slightest breeze would cause it to billow out. When annoyed, or deep in concentration, this animal stood stiff-legged, mane erect, and the brush pushed out in a straight line level with its back. The natives say that when seen standing like this in long grass at night, with the moon appearing to shine clear through the outline, then 'ghost wolf' is a perfect name for it.

The more common European or Canadian timber wolves have always been a popular draw to the public.

As the visitor stands watching them in their open paddock at the Zoo, or in their wooded area of Whipsnade,
he may have silent thoughts as to how he might behave
if he were to be surrounded by a ravenously hungry pack
of these animals creeping forward yard by yard before
the final onslaught. Yet I know people who thought
of wolves as only the most docile and friendly of
animals.

Some forty years ago, anyone walking from one part
of the Zoo to another before the gardens opened at
9am might turn a corner to be suddenly confronted by
as many as four wolves straining on link chains held
by a man who considered he was the friend of all wolves
and could converse with them in their own language.
Most days in the week, he would harness up the wolves
and take them on a tour of the gardens. Afterwards he
would sit for anything up to an hour in their cage,
hardly visible under cover of the big grey bodies that
swarmed over him. I once saw him flat on his back,
with two sets of wet slobbering jaws inches from his
throat, but he was so much at ease that he asked me
the time. Though he had been granted permission by
the authorities to indulge in his passion to be close to
wolves, providing that any mishap was his own res-
ponsibility, the menagerie staff had definite views of
their own and were not slow to voice them. It sometimes
happened, for instance, that when the keepers were
cleaning the rocky surface of Monkey Hill, having
first driven the thirty or forty Hamadryas baboons to
the far side, the animals came swarming back again,
frightened by the approach of the wolves, and the

keepers would have to make a hasty exit. Planned
and agreed routes eventually smoothed things over,
but you could never be quite sure about those wolves.

A peer of the realm not only housed his two wolves,
Helen and Sheik, at the Zoo but came to visit them.
He would take them for walks and even on one occasion
took them by taxi to call on his mother, who lived
nearby. Whether the taxi-driver thought his passengers
were dogs or whether a fat tip helped allay his fears,
I never knew, but Helen and Sheik arrived back safely,
and so did his lordship—and there was no report of any
cabbie's mutilated body being found. No such excur-
sions are possible nowadays, as regulations forbid any
animal being taken from the Zoo for any but the most
essential purposes.

6
Elephant Walks

JUMBO

Why 'Jumbo' and where does the name originate? Try putting 'Mumbo' in front of 'Jumbo' and you will say, 'Ahh, African elephant—African witchcraft', and you will be absolutely right. It was way back in 1865 that a young African elephant arrived at the London Zoo. His chances of survival at first appeared remote. He was in a deplorable condition and extremely ill, so much so that it was one man's job to attend to his needs. The man destined to become almost as well known as his small charge was a Keeper Scott whose task, quite apart from his nursing duties, could not have been easy, for it is a well-known fact that the African elephant does not usually take kindly to training and discipline, and the male of the species is the more likely to prove troublesome. Thanks to Scott, the condition of young Jumbo greatly improved and as time went on he accepted the man as a master who must be obeyed. However, as he grew older and bigger, no one, apart from Scott, dare approach him without risking serious injury.

With Scott around to pacify and control him, he was coaxed into accepting a saddle on his back and eventually seemed to enjoy carrying children and grown-ups

for rides up and down Elephant Walk. Soon his fame
spread and people came from all parts of the country to
see him; I believe Sir Winston Churchill as a lad was
one of many famous people who took their first elephant
ride on Jumbo. As Jumbo grew to 11ft in height, he
became more and more of a risk. His tusks were now
strong enough to cause havoc in his den and on one
occasion he broke off both of them in his frenzy. His
fame had by now spread to America, and London Zoo
accepted an offer from Mr Barnum, one of the greatest
showmen of all time, for the huge animal to be sent to
him. Letters of protest poured into London Zoo; children went to bed crying at night, and Scott himself
pleaded with the officials to change their minds. He
suggested that if Jumbo went away, Alice, the only
other elephant at the Zoo, would probably pine for
him. Of course, the public seized upon this as further
evidence that to send away an animal who, in the
seventeen years he had been at the Zoo, had become
such a favourite with visitors was wrong, and by causing
distress to another animal the decision bordered on
cruelty. After consideration by the Zoo Council it was
decided that the worries concerning Alice were un-
founded, an opinion which later proved to be correct.
When the day arrived for Jumbo to be boxed up, all
the efforts of Barnum's representative failed to entice
him into the travelling box and Scott saw no reason to
give a helping hand.

Day after day for several weeks efforts were renewed
to get the animal securely crated, until Barnum decided
that if he wanted Jumbo he must take Scott as well,

for one would not part from the other. When Scott learned he could accompany his old pal, the job was completed the same day and the journey to London Docks began. The huge box, drawn by teams of dray horses, made its way through streets lined with people who had come to wave goodbye to the animal whose name was a byword. They do say the children cried as loudly as the parents booed and sleep did not come easily that night. When the crate was hoisted aboard ship, Scott sat on top of it with the tip of Jumbo's trunk in his hand, now and again giving a tit-bit and assuring the big fellow that all was well. On arrival in New York, Scott walked at Jumbo's head as they made their way to Madison Square and for the next three years the two were seldom apart. When Jumbo appeared in the circus, Scott was right beside him, and while the show was on the road they shared the same box. Jumbo died in a train accident, but is immortalised in the affectionate nickname given to all elephants by children and grown-ups alike.

CHANG AND KELLY

While I was working for a short while in the sanatorium, Chang, a young Indian bull elephant, arrived. Aged about seven, he weighed something like a ton. Each day he was brought out from his stable for exercise, his front legs shackled to prevent him having too much freedom of movement, but allowing him to walk in comfort. His mahout, San Dwe, or Sandy as he quickly became known, was patience itself in the handling of his charge and soon taught Chang to play a mouth-organ, but at the same time he was firm in his instruction to us to keep well away from the animal. Sandy once said to me, 'One day this will be a bad elephant'. When I asked how he knew, he replied, 'I tell by his eye, sometime it red'.

Then came the day when Chang was to be moved to his new home in the Elephant House, which in those days was in the Middle Gardens on the south side of the canal. Sandy was not available to take charge of the situation, so it was decided to call in old Kelly, the largest of the female elephants, who was placid by nature and seemed best able to reassure the youngster. Soon after 6.30am Kelly, with Charlie, her keeper, riding on her neck, stood waiting whilst a long chain was attached to her harness, then linked up to Chang's shackles. It was thought Kelly's slow progress and her strength to keep Chang moving, if he became stubborn and wished to stop, would make things go smoothly and at first everything went according to plan. To get from the sanatorium in the Main Gardens to the Middle Gardens, it was necessary to go through a tunnel beneath the outer circle of Regent's Park. The circular shape of the tunnel made it essential for any elephant to keep strictly to the centre when passing through, other-wise the man on top could be swept from his perch.

Charlie was doing his best to guide Kelly on to a correct course when Chang suddenly screamed and began playing up. Kelly had been through that tunnel hundreds of times with the rest of the riding elephants, but on this occasion she really panicked. Perhaps she

was getting fed up with playing nursemaid, or knowing
she was nearing home decided to hurry; anyway Chang's
sudden scream from behind set her off. As the pace became too fast for his comfort, Chang bellowed even
louder in protest, and the louder he bellowed the faster
Kelly went through that tunnel, while poor Charlie lay
flat on her head to avoid being crushed. Even the in-
cline on the far side failed to slow her down. She was
going so fast she was unable to turn at the top and
continued right on through the shrubbery before sight-
ing the railings that kept children away from the towpath and the water of the canal. She swung away from
danger, but Chang was unable to pull up and went
clean through the railings, across the towpath and had
a brief ducking before he was dragged out again by the
still rampaging Kelly. Charlie, tense and white-faced,
was trying all the time to get her to slow down. Only
when she found she had not got to get through the
Giraffe House doors did some semblance of order
return. Somehow or other the mission was completed
to the relief of all concerned, especially old Charlie.

Chang's stay at the Zoo did not last very long, for
he soon gave cause for concern that Sandy's opinion
would at some time or other be proved correct. His
temper got worse and he was sold to another zoo willing
to take a chance with him.

SALLY

Some eight years after that escapade, there was another
case of an elephant putting on speed and this time

Page 75 Edmund Purdom and Trevor Howard visit the Zoo; (*above*) with the elephants and their keeper, Buck Jones; (*below*) in conversation with a sealion

Page 76 Perfect manners from Rabiu on being introduced to HRH Princess Margaret

Sally was the culprit. On this not very busy day, she
and Ranee needed to be prodded forward more than
usual as they wended their way up and down the length
of Elephant Walk giving rides to the few children
present and there was hardly anyone on the sidelines
to feed them with buns. With half an hour of riding
time still to go, Sally carried three children and the
father of one of them on the outward journey, then
turned as usual to make her way back to the high platform steps where the passengers were to be taken off.
Suddenly she made up her mind that she had had
enough and her walking pace rapidly increased, she
went between the steps, but would not stop and the
keepers had no time to unload as she rushed by. Most
of the staff on duty in the riding square did all they
could to assist Buck Jones, her rider, to slow her down,
but she made for home at a fair old lick with her
precious cargo still aboard. The horrifying thought in
the minds of the keepers, who were running full out to
keep up, was that if Sally wavered from a straight line
through the centre of the tunnel, the saddle and its
passengers would be swept from her back. As she
approached the opening, her course was anything but
true; then, at the very last moment, she swung to the
centre. Up the slope on the other side she went, then
turned right and trumpeted loudly as she sighted her
home. Our fear at this moment was that she would try
to make straight for her stall without waiting for the
saddle to be removed, but she slowed down and finally
stopped right under the pulley which was used to lift
off the heavy gear. Buck made her kneel so that we could

D

reach the safety straps and drag the children down. We made a joke of it, telling them they had had an extra long ride for their money. The kids were marvellous, regarding the whole thing as something to talk about at home, but poor Dad looked as though he was about to be sick. The overseer, who had caught us up, gave orders to quickly unsaddle Sally and get her inside. However, Buck, now in possession of his second wind, had other views. 'Let her get away with this and she may try it again. It's back to the square to finish the job.' So we tightened up the straps again. Sally stood up, was turned round and made to go all the way back. For the remaining twenty minutes or so Ranee stood quietly on the side watching as Sally paraded up and down, this time with four young keepers on her back. When five o'clock struck, there were at least four very relieved minds. I know, because mine was one of them.

7
Open to Visitors

DISTINGUISHED COMPANY

The London Zoo is under Royal Charter and, ever since it opened in 1828, members of the Royal Family have shown a keen interest in its welfare. In my early days, the two little princesses, Elizabeth and Margaret Rose, came in the care of a governess to see what I believe was their favourite attraction, the Chimpanzees' Tea Party. The antics of these born comedians brought obvious delight to the royal children and they came back several times for a repeat show. Towards the end of my time at the Zoo, Her Majesty the Queen, accompanied by Prince Philip and Princess Margaret, went on a short tour of the gardens prior to opening the new Clore Pavilion for small mammals. It was a proud moment for me when the royal party paused to admire Rabiu, the cheetah, whom I had led to one of the lower walks so that they could get a close view of him. On an earlier visit, Princess Margaret and her son, Viscount Lindley, had watched Rabiu lapping milk from a dish.

I had already met Prince Philip on three occasions: once when I was one of a small group chosen to sit down to lunch with him before he took the chair at a Zoo council meeting; again when, as president, he presented me with the Society Medal for long and

meritorious service; and also when he performed the
ceremony at the opening of the new bridge across the
canal which runs through the gardens. Now I found
myself placed next to him at lunch and I must confess
I had butterflies in my stomach. However, in no time
at all, I felt at ease and was joining in the conversation
on my favourite subject—animals.

In about the middle 1950s, we had in the North
Mammal House a lovely female leopard from North
Africa, called Sheba, who had been presented as a
gift to Sir Winston Churchill. Another of his presenta-
tions, a young male lion, was in the Lion House some
distance away and, when it was learned that the great
man planned to visit the Zoo, I was instructed to take
Sheba over there for the day, so that the two animals
could be under the same roof. The head keeper was
there to answer questions about the lion, and then it was
my turn to introduce Sheba. To prove how friendly
she was, I called her up close to the bars, then put my
arm through to fondle her behind the ears. In his gruff
but kindly way Sir Winston asked if I considered it
possible for him to try it. Well! for one thing there
was no link netting in front of the cages, just upright
bars with a six-inch span between; also Sheba was in
a strange temporary home surrounded by stranger
smells and noises. But my confidence in her was such
that, after again demonstrating the correct way to
caress her and keeping my hand close in case she should
turn her head, I invited Sir Winston to rub her neck.
This he did with all the surety of an old hand. One of
my most treasured possessions is an album with photo-

graphs showing the two of us deep in conversation about leopards in general and Sheba in particular.

CAT'S EYE VIEW

If only the animal could tell us what he sees when the two-legged human mammal approaches him! How for instance would he describe a man like Jimmy Dyrenforth, who had been a regular visitor to the North Mammal House many years before the arrival of his beloved Mickey. His soft American drawl and quiet unassuming manner made him a natural when it came to winning the confidence of an animal, especially one of the larger cats. As Jimmy slowly moved towards it, hand outstretched, soothing words audible only to the creature in front of him, he seemed to mesmerise it. He believed the animals knew he would never harm them, and that they responded in kind. This was a faith I never quite knew in anyone else, though a few came mighty close.

Another interesting study from the animal's point of view would be the late Sir Malcolm Sargent. He was a regular visitor to Prince, who was quite at home with him, but Sir Malcolm was usually accompanied by up to a dozen of his adoring young female pupils, half of whom were obviously scared of the animal, and who were all the time jostling with each other to be closest to the maestro. Quite often Prince had to move quickly to avoid having his tail trodden on and in no time at all he would get fed up with it all and walk away. As he looked at Sir Malcolm, I can only describe his expression as saying, 'Come on your own next time and stay as long as you like.'

Victor McLaglen, the one-time tough guy of Hollywood films, could not be persuaded to enter Prince's cage, even though the remainder of his party thoroughly enjoyed themselves. Poor Prince sat in the circle of his visitors with a look of wonderment on his face as he gazed at the big man outside, 'Surely you cannot be scared of me!' Victor's expression seemed to say 'Anything on two legs I can cope with. You I am not so sure about'. In the circumstances this was the sensible attitude to adopt, for most animals quickly sense if a person is apprehensive and more often than not will cash in on the knowledge, if only to the extent of riotous play. I have only the greatest sympathy for people who have this fear of animals; however much they try to hide it they always seem to be singled out for extra attention by the animal concerned. Whether caged or domestic, all animals seem to have this knack of knowing who will provide most fun and the only advice I can offer the victim is to keep quite still, and grin and bear it.

There is another kind of individual who cannot listen to advice of any kind: he of the loud voice and demonstrative manner, who knows it all or thinks he does. This type, luckily for the keepers, is not such a frequent visitor to the Zoo these days, mainly because of the feeding ban. We at the North Mammal House came to know a few such people very well, and on Sunday mornings you could almost set your watch by them. All would be peaceful and then the silence was suddenly shattered by a loud, 'Come on then!' This to be followed by an invitation to the visitors within earshot, 'You watch this. He knows me because I always bring him food.' The carrier bag would be produced and most times the animal would move forward to accept a morsel of meat. This was the chance for the loud-voiced one to show off his talents as an orator and, as his admirers gathered round, the animal's history would be flung to the four corners of the gardens. It was always a source of wonder to me that when the animal, having seen that the one piece of meat was to be his lot, moved as far away as possible from the human dynamo, this rebuff never seemed to discourage him in the least. Next Sunday on the dot came the repeat performance. I knew my charges well enough to be able to read their minds, and given a chance to contribute to a book on human behaviour they would say, 'Look, mate, we only tolerate you for what you bring. Our real friends are the people who come regularly and show us genuine affection without the aid of tit-bits.'

The top floor of the Regent restaurant was in great demand for wedding receptions, Rotary Club gatherings, and other celebrations, and on these occasions an animal display was usually put on for the guests. Coochie, the fennec fox, was the ideal foil for the chimpanzee, another regular entertainer who spent most of the evening in the arms of people anxious to be photographed with a companion out of the ordinary. Naturally the chimp was the cause of much merriment as the cocktails were being served and the 'wise guys' were full of cracks in their attempts to impress the ladies with their wit. I generally found that the more reserved people would leave the chimp and move to another corner of the room to talk to the keepers in charge of the bush baby, the potto, the cockatoo, a harmless snake and delightful little Coochie. During the summer season such parties could be held on the Fellows Lawn and then perhaps a young elephant, llama, gazelle, even a cheetah would be there for presentation.

DRAWING THE CROWDS

About the middle of the 1930s one of the popular Sunday newspapers ran a series of articles, written in slightly humorous vein, but also very informative, about the animals at the London Zoo. Quite often the author would call on a Friday and say 'I've been all round the Zoo and no one seems to have a story. You've not let me down yet, what about it?' So we would take a stroll along the passage and stop at a cage where the resident seemed to fit the bill. My friend would get me talking, popping in the odd question here and there, and over a cup of tea in the staff room the story for the next edition would be born.

At that time you hardly ever read a newspaper without coming across something or other to do with the Zoo. One hot summer day a freelance photographer and I put our heads together to such good purpose that he was taken on the staff of a daily newspaper. This man, carrying a large camera case slung around his neck, came up and spoke to me about the chances of getting some good pictures of a group of bear cubs, two brown and two Syrian, who shared one extra large outside

Page 85 (above) A still from the film *The Berlin Story*, in which the author and Prince, the cheetah, took part; *(below)* Sir Winston Churchill visiting Sheba, a lovely female leopard from North Africa, which had been presented to him

Page 86 (above) Coochie, the dainty and utterly feminine little fennec fox; *(below)* bear cubs having a fine game with a home-made shower

Page 87 The author getting to know four young chimpanzees by daily contact before escorting them to their new home at Wellington Zoo, New Zealand

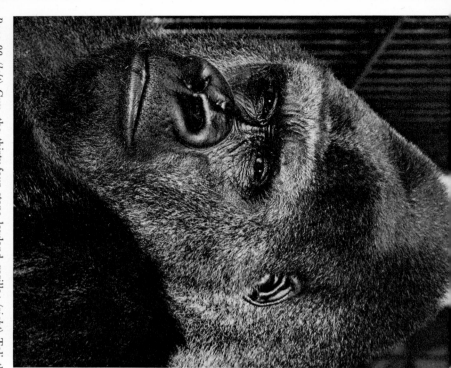

Page 88 (*left*) Guy, the thirty-four stone lowland gorilla; (*right*) Toli the orang-utan showing off Bulu, the first baby orang-utan to be born and reared in Great Britain

den and whose antics kept visitors highly amused all day long. I explained that because of their frolicsome nature it would be difficult to keep them still long enough to photograph, unless we provided some sort of attraction to hold their attention. A shower bath seemed ideal, so I looked around for the appropriate props: a watering can, complete with rose sprayer, a length of hosepipe, some wire and a tin of sweetened milk. The pipe was laid on the ground and, of course, the cubs needed no prompting to drag it around the cage and picture No 1 was taken. The pipe was then rescued, fixed to a water tap in the corner, the tap smeared with the sweetened milk and some lively activity in and around this area resulted in picture No 2. Then the watering can, tilted well forward, was tied to an upright iron support bar, which received the milk treatment up to a height level with the can. The cubs' efforts to climb the bar in order to reach the milk at the top had the crowd shrieking with laughter—picture No 3. One end of the hosepipe was then placed in the suspended watering can and one of the cubs very obligingly stood up on his hind legs with one paw on the can long enough for picture No 4 to be taken. Once more back to the tap with the pipe still fixed; a short wait until a paw was touching the actual tap and, presto, No 5. As soon as I really did turn on the water, the hose carried it up to the watering can and the rose provided an effective shower which simply delighted the cubs. They splashed and rolled, came out, shook themselves and dashed back under the shower, and all the while the people round the cage were roaring with laughter.

After the photographer departed, I resumed normal duties until much later in the evening when a violent thunderstorm caused me to take cover inside. At the height of the storm a taxicab drew up at the rear of the building in the main road and my newfound friend with the camera shouted that he had taken the shower bath pictures to Fleet Street, the paper had been delighted and he himself had been taken on the staff. In next morning's paper, a sequence of six pictures showed the bears supposedly rigging up a shower for themselves, and it gave me a great sense of satisfaction to sit in the tube on the way to work and listen to comments and words of praise. Such publicity has a very marked influence on the number of paying customers passing through the turnstiles at Regent's Park. When Brumas, the polar bear cub, was born, the papers carried pictures and articles about her for months afterwards. That year, the total number of visitors rocketed to over three million for the first and only time. Goldie, the golden eagle, had sat high on her perch in the Birds of Prey Aviary for years, without a second glance from the public, until one day she escaped through an open door and remained free in the nearby park for a week or so. Pictures of the efforts made to recapture her had London divided in its views as to whether or not she should be allowed to remain free. When she was caught and brought back home, there were long queues wanting to see what she looked like. Fifty thousand people would be a moderate estimate of the extra number who turned up.

Once in a while a real crowd puller, like the mating

of Chi-Chi of London Zoo with An-An from Moscow Zoo, will bring in much extra revenue. The hopes and beliefs that the two giant pandas would fall in love resulted in the most extravagant arrangements being made to ensure that their romance had every chance of succeeding. The future of any progeny arriving after the marriage was also agreed upon, but never at any time were the prospects even hopeful. Chi-Chi and An-An ignored each other completely; on the few occasions they came close together, they showed quite plainly they were not made for each other. Homesickness was not an excuse, for they shared the same quarters, first in Moscow, then in London, but all to no avail. The romantically minded humans, however, never gave up hope and large crowds turned up every day to watch the progress of the courtship, though it is a safe bet to say very few of them could tell which was which.

8

Animals In and Out of Cages

The London Zoo has made admirable attempts during the last twenty years to improve its physical image and to comply with generally agreed standards of accommodation for animals, not only to show them off to the best advantage but to satisfy their needs of comfort. The Cotton Terrace was the first major step in this direction, a project which consisted of dismantling the old giraffe house, the zebra house, the stables and works department. A new palatial building was erected around the giraffes, giving them a high, warm, draught-proof home. Wings were added to house yak, water buffalo and zebra on one side, and llama, alpacca and vicuna on the other. The outside exercise yards from one end to the other are surrounded by a moat populated by hundreds of goldfish. Down the steps to the pens below you will come to the exalted Père David deer, now extinct except for those in captivity, and the equally large but not so impressive red deer. Move along and you can watch the black buck speeding around their paddock showing off to some of their bigger cousins. Full marks from me for this new accommodation, although perhaps next summer it will be necessary to drag another venturesome youngster from the water and rush him inside to the keepers' room to be dried out.

Opposite on the other bank of the canal, the Snowdon Aviary rears up to the sky. It permits more or less free flight for birds and a walk-through path for the public, but when it was first built many visitors asked the keepers what it was supposed to be. Perhaps it has proved its worth by now, but I could never get enthusiastic about it.

The Clore Pavilion for small mammals has many advantages over the old house, and the breeding records have been greatly improved. The birth of fennec foxes in this country is a pleasing item of news that I had given up hope of hearing. In the old days the rodent house, which then stood on the north bank of the canal, was a mixture of good news and bad news. The bad news was that the glass roof and sides of the building let in so much light that, during the bright summer days when the gardens were most thickly populated with visitors, only about twenty-five per cent of the stock were viewable. The rest were buried deep in the bedding of their sleeping boxes snoozing away the daylight hours. As the light faded and closing time approached, they all began to look alive and show themselves, but to a much diminished audience. The most popular animals living there were the Galagos or bush babies. Because these were among the last to wake, many people were denied the sight of their small fluffy bodies, long tails and enormous solemn-looking brown eyes. The good news was that the keeper-in-charge, George Graves, in addition to being a most knowledgable man, was a soft touch for children. Many a time I have seen him busily cleaning out cages when a tearful little girl came up to him, asking why she could not see the bush babies. After a little by-play, he would unlock a cage, put in his hand and lift out a sleepy, completely relaxed bush baby. The child's face would light up with amazement at being the recipient of so much favour and, if she listened to and obeyed instructions, not only was she able to stroke the soft furry bundle, but actually to cradle it in her own arms. Soon more children would be eager to stretch out a hand to touch the treasure and George would be surrounded by a small crowd of mums and dads, some seeking advice as to the best methods of keeping bush babies as pets. He would patiently explain that because the one on view was half asleep it allowed itself to be handled, but after dark when fully awake the same animal would resent such liberties being taken and would bite.

In the present building most animals are on view all day long, but alas cannot be touched. In their underground moonlight world, with only the minimum artificial lighting, these nocturnal residents come out to play, although it is daytime. After the visitors leave, extra lighting floods the area and the animals retire to their beds for the night, or should I say day? On the whole, I like this arrangement, but have my doubts about keeping small cats behind glass with no outside run to provide variety. The cat is a creature of the open, needing to feel the sun and the wind, even the rain on its face. I recall how happy they used to be to remain in their outside cages during a light shower, for this must have been an easy way of getting a fur-cleaning freshener. If a rainstorm came on they would bolt inside, dry off as only they knew how, then reappear outside when the sun shone. Keep a cat in, say, a transportation box, even a large one, and you will find that, unless a good supply of fresh air gets to it, the coat will soon become damp and matted, and the cat itself begin to look miserable. The air conditioning is undoubtedly of the best in the Clore Pavilion, but I still think at least a glimpse of the sun and the feel of a sprinkling of rain would be much appreciated by the inmates.

During my long stay at the Zoo the elephants had three different homes. The one already in existence when I arrived was a red brick building with a slanting roof and a huge loft for storing hay, straw and foodstuffs. Inside there were separate stalls, one per elephant, with thick oak posts in front and a narrow safety barrier to protect the public. In the winter months, the place hardly ever appeared to be dry and the atmosphere was not improved by the numerous rats living in luxury up above. There was room for an elephant to walk from its stall through the door at the back and out into the exercise yard. On riding days the big animals walked from the yard through an iron gate and round to the front of the house to be saddled up. A real problem arose in the early 1930s when the biggest elephant of all became ill and died rather suddenly. A large crane would have been needed to lift the entire carcass, but there was not enough room for such machinery to operate and it was necessary to bisect the body and remove half at a time.

The second home could scarcely be called an elephant 'house' for the animals stood on a round island surrounded by a dry moat, with only the sky above for a roof. There they stood all day and every day, doing very well in the way of tit-bits, for they were always great favourites with the public. The stables, or sleeping quarters, were below ground and each night the animals walked down the slope that led to the highly piled straw beds. I cannot honestly say I favoured these conditions; for one thing, during wet weather, the rain would run down the slope and, with little or no air conditioning, the underground stalls seemed to me damp, dark and dismal. More than once the staff had to combat flooding, with restless elephants bellowing a protest at the discomfort, swinging this way and that to avoid the water, and all in a very confined space. The wonder to me is that no serious accident occurred; the few times I had occasion to go down below my business was very soon completed. When big Dixie walked by, you flattened yourself against the wall, drew a deep breath and held it.

Today the elephants can be found living in palatial surroundings next door to the lion house in the Middle Gardens. Even the nameplate, 'Elephant and Rhino Pavilion', suggests grandeur and though its design is unusual the building has much to commend it. Inside the viewing hall the circular style enables visitors to stand on one spot turning slowly to get a clear look at all the inhabitants. The high-roofed, warm, dry and altogether very pleasing interior seems to be much appreciated by the inmates, especially the rhinos, who, by way of showing their gratitude, produced a bonny bouncing baby for the first time in the history of the Zoo. People enjoying a walk through Regent's Park have good reason to rejoice over the change of venue, for the elephants can be clearly seen in their outside quarters. One of the conditions of the Zoo's Royal Charter is that a certain number of animals must be in sight of people using the park and it is difficult to imagine a more popular choice to meet the requirements.

A new enclosure has been built to accommodate Guy, the gorilla, and his female companion, where the spacious, continental-style exterior allows them freedom of movement. Guy, who weighs something in the region of 34 stone, had previously occupied a cage in the ape section of the monkey house, and there were many who protested bitterly at the apparent lack of space. I have only admiration for those animal lovers who speak out against something which offends their ideals. They had the evidence of their own eyes and formed their own opinions. Perhaps now the change has been effected I can give my own views, which were formed after taking into consideration a few facts that may have been overlooked by the critics.

Guy is now about twenty-six years old. He came to the Zoo when a baby of five months, his body weight being 35lb. His devoted friend was Laurie Smith, head keeper of the monkey house, who made a daily practice of staging a lengthy playtime session with his young charge. A special watch was kept and the health of the valuable youngster was given top priority. In those

E

days keeping a gorilla in captivity was a chancy business. Still fresh in the minds of the older keepers was the
very short survival of Moina and Mok, two mature
animals who had the benefit of specially-made, large
quarters and all that was best in the way of food (I
myself can vouch for the quality of the chicken broth).
Ten or so keepers danced attendance on them, to open
and shut the protective screen, which either let in
sun or shut out the cold, and yet both gorillas died without becoming really established.

As Guy grew bigger and stronger, some hefty
thumps were exchanged when Smithy and he rolled
and wrestled around. These sessions, always in great
demand by the visitors, went on until Smithy found he
was giving away too much weight and threw in the
towel to end the unequal contest. Even so, he continued
to slap his old mate around in the service passage at the
rear, but now there were bars between them. Guy's
strength was such that, had he chosen to grab and hold
Smithy's arms, he could have torn both limbs from
their sockets, but the close observer, often myself, noted
how the gorilla was careful not to risk harming his
friend. One of my lasting memories was the sight of two
heads, one four times larger than the other, placed so
close together that the noses were actually touching,
while a grape held in the mouth of one was gently removed by the lips of the other and swallowed. I also
remember discussing with Smithy a newspaper article
supporting the claims of those who demanded larger
quarters and a mate for Guy. Poor Smithy, always a wor-
rier at the slightest hint that anything was less than 100-

per-cent perfection in the monkey house, looked upon this latest outcry as a personal attack upon himself. 'People don't understand, Jim', he said to me in that soft, sincere voice of his. 'Guy has grown to regard the limited space as good protection for him, keeping people at a distance, and not too large an area to defend. He came, as you remember, just a baby, now he is fully grown. Apart from minor ailments in his infant days, he has always enjoyed the best of health, so there can't be much wrong with his accommodation. Also Moina and Mok had each other for company, but this did not make for longer life.' My view is that, if Guy was suffering in any way, the loudest protest of all would have come from his one great friend, a man whose judgement on the subject of apes I would back against anyone.

In the Autumn of 1972 I saw Guy's new home for the first time. Now that Smithy is, like myself, eligible for the pensioners' reunion party each year, I could not get his views on the change, but another keeper, hearing that I was going across to the enclosure, said, 'I doubt if you will find Guy outside. He spends all his time in the smaller inside den, although the female is nearly always outside.' This proved to be the case and my mind went back to Laurie Smith who might pardonably have said, 'I told you so.'

During the whole period of my service at the London Zoo, the times an animal succeeded in breaking free from its cage were so few and far between that it is hard to recall them. In my early days, there were those escapades by the monkey from the sanatorium and the chimpanzees from the isolation ward; and, much later, I remember when the chimp Cholmondeley almost made up his mind to go for a ride on a No 74 bus, before deciding that the open spaces of Regent's Park offered a better chance of freedom. He made the wrong choice, for he was back home in no time at all and never looked like approaching the record afterwards set up by Goldie, the eagle.

Ideas and plans for making a zoo escape-proof have been put forward for many years past, but the ideal solution has yet to be found. A wide, deep moat filled with water encircling the whole area has been suggested, but this would not deter those animals who can swim and, in a hard winter when it was covered with ice, would not be much of a handicap to a would-be escaper. A moat without water also has snags. It is quite possible that a 20ft drop on to a concrete base would result in many serious accidents, even fatal ones, to members of the public. Such a moat might prevent escapes, but could be a danger to the animals too. In the 1960s, poor Dixie, the Zoo's largest elephant, was trapped in one surrounding her enclosure. It was never known how she toppled into it, but she became tightly wedged against the perimeter wall and all efforts to release her failed. Her leg had been broken in the fall and she could not respond to the attempts to help her stand up. Lying as she was on her side, the pressure on her heart proved too great and she died.

As regards the number of escapes, London Zoo has a remarkably low record, considering the size of its collection in comparison with smaller menageries. All too often nowadays, you read in the newspapers about animals which have got loose from a privately owned zoo or a circus. Two recent incidents concerned young lions which escaped from their quarters; in one case the animals were cornered and recaptured fairly easily by the use of tranquilliser darts, but in the other the lions had to be shot dead because of possible danger to nearby schoolchildren. Such happenings must surely open up the whole question of the licensing laws covering animal confinement. With the ever-growing number of places operating under the name of 'zoo', many of them housing a selection of species in totally insecure cages and staffed very often by young boys and girls, control should be considerably tightened.

An animal seen roaming free in the southern counties of England in 1967 gained widespread publicity and gave rise to a mystery that has never been solved. The cause of the hue and cry was said to be a puma, but until it had been identified by a responsible person I kept an open mind on the subject. According to newspaper reports, the phantom was sighted first in one area and then, almost simultaneously, in another many miles away. Eventually a plaster cast of a pug mark, said to be a footprint of the suspect marauder, was brought to the Zoo for me to identify. With the assistance of my huge friend, Sabre, who obligingly produced an authentic puma print in a deep pan filled with wet sand, I was able to show that, in size, shape and pattern, the cast impression was not that of a puma. For a time the story lost some of its news value, then a report came in that the New Forest was now the haunt of the mystery cat on the loose. One vital piece of evidence was missing, as far as I was concerned. Horseflesh is most decidedly the favourite dish of the puma, and yet there were no reports of any New Forest ponies being killed for food. To be surrounded by such a wealth of good eating and yet not yield to temptation, what kind of a puma was that?

9

With Animals Abroad

VOYAGE TO NEW ZEALAND

Early in 1957 I had been promoted to the rank of
Senior Head Keeper and in October that year I was
given the opportunity to visit New Zealand. The Wellington Zoo had arranged for the purchase from us of a
young male giraffe and four chimpanzees, and I was
chosen to escort them on their way. Sailing day was one
of hazy sunshine during the morning and then a thick
blanket of fog as darkness fell. At 10pm we began to
inch our way slowly down the river from the London
Docks. The ship's fog siren was blaring out every few
seconds, and the answering blasts from other vessels
combined to make an unearthly din all the way to
Greenwich. Knowing how nervous and highly strung a
giraffe is, I sat alongside his high-roofed travelling box,
talking quietly and doing my best to calm him. But
soon after we entered the Channel, he went down in his
box and I knew I had trouble on my hands, for once
down in such circumstances a giraffe will seldom make
any effort to stand. The crew were wonderful; they
made strong canvas slings, which I somehow managed
to get around his big body, and then a dozen of us
heaved and strained to hoist him up. It needed only a
little help on his part, but he would not budge. My

only hope was that, as we steamed into clearer, warmer air, with the roof of his box removed, he might stand up by himself to view his new surroundings. But even this possibility was denied me, for suddenly the order was given to change course to Falmouth, as the ship had developed some trouble or other. As soon as we docked I phoned the Zoo. The following morning our own vet came and another attempt was made to get the giraffe to stand, this time with the help of the ship's winch. It was hopeless, however, and in the midst of it all, the giraffe dropped his head, gave a deep sigh and died.

The rest of the four-week trip turned out to be one of the most trouble free. The first ten days passed very quickly; chimps are fairly good travellers, and I was kept busy feeding my charges three times a day, cleaning and disinfecting their boxes, providing their milk drinks and taking them for walks around the deck morning and afternoon. The slight coughing which had troubled all the chimps immediately following the fog went completely in the brilliant sunshine and the daily dose of medicine was no longer necessary.

The eight passengers aboard were highly amused by the antics of the 'Fabulous Four', the title they bestowed on Tommy, Teddy, Jimmy and Mickey, and a careful watch had to be kept on the nature and amount of foodstuffs offered as a reward for some comical turns. On the morning of Tuesday, 5 November, I sensed that I had become the object of more than usual interest and when I learned we were to cross the International Date Line at 4pm that day I feared the worst. So I suggested to the captain that perhaps the passengers would enjoy watching a chimpanzees' tea party and that he might sit down at the table with the chimps so that some pictures could be taken. These would, I said, be treasured by his grandchildren in years to come. He readily agreed and asked what time he should present himself. I said, 'Sixteen hundred hours today, sir! That is the time they sit down in London'. Thus it was that for the first and probably the last time on board ship the 'Crossing the Bar' ceremony consisted of a chimps' tea party with the skipper sitting at their table and being served the same rations.

On Friday, 1 November, we followed the coastline of Venezula round to Cristobal, the gateway to the Panama Canal. For the next two days I was treated to a marvellous display of tiny flying fish in their thousands, taking off and alighting on waves, you would think their frail bodies would be smashed to pieces; but the timing and judgement of each operation was perfection itself and completed with absolute safety. We saw porpoises and pelicans, meal times often being delayed as the passengers lined the ship's rail to watch their activities.

On the Sunday morning, we picked up our pilot and began to wind our way through the waterways on the canal. For all of seven hours I experienced the thrill of a lifetime, as first we entered the lock at Gatun where, in three separate hoists of 70ft each and with the help of a small engine attached to each side of the ship, we were able to look back over the stern from a height of 210ft, and marvel at the ingenuity of man. After clearing the lock, we continued through a channel of water so narrow that, as we passed the *Southern Prince* going in the opposite direction on her way to London, we could almost shake hands with her passengers at the rail. Thousands of small, gloriously coloured birds were singing in the palm trees on the small islands just alongside and, if there is no fairyland, then this must be the nearest thing to it. The second lock was the Pedro Miguel. All the way down the scenery was magnificent: some stretches very reminiscent of the Norfolk Broads; others were high ledges lining the banks on either side of the sheer rock face of the Calebra Cut. The Miraflores Lock was cleared and, after dropping the pilot at Bilbao, we entered the Pacific. On 21 November, we reached Wellington, New Zealand, and the chimps were all asleep in their new home soon after 9pm. Three days later, as a special treat for the many visitors who had come to see them, the chimps sat down at the table with two of Wellington Zoo's female chimps and behaved just as though they were on the lawn at Regent's Park. If any proof were needed as to how they would settle down, here it was, and even more pleasing was the fact that they liked their new keeper on sight, and he them.

New Zealand has a reputation for its hospitality and I welcome the chance to add my own tribute to those wonderfully friendly people, who did all in their power to make my short stay as enjoyable as possible. I even took morning tea with the Lord Mayor at the Town Hall. I travelled home by air across Australia, Africa and India and thus completed a round-the-world trip. In Sydney, I was able to visit Toronga Park Zoo,

which has the most beautiful setting of any I have
visited. It is built so high that you look down on the
shipping entering and leaving that busy harbour. I
found special interest in being able to see the Koala
bears and the collection of birds of paradise, known to be
the best in the world. Above all, I remember the sight of
some nine or ten cheetahs in a long enclosure; although
sectioned off, every dividing gate was open so that they
were able to intermingle freely and choose their own
companions. The fresh clean air and a climate so
different from our own no doubt had a lot to do with
the cats' perfect condition.

ZOOS IN EUROPE

In 1960 I was one of a party of fourteen from London
and Whipsnade sent to study methods of animal man-
agement adopted by zoos in Holland, Germany,
Switzerland and Belgium. We discovered that the
presentation of, say, lions was very different on the
Continent to the rather small holding units in London.
They favour the open area with sheer, unclimbable
rock at the back and sides, and a water moat as a safety
barrier at the front. Frankfurt Zoo was the most impressive, for the grass verge leading down to the moat
is sloped, so that the public approaching the spot are
unaware of the water and at first imagine there is nothing to keep the lions from walking out to meet them.
Everywhere the accent seemed to be on space, with
fewer exhibits but more room for each; this trend will,
I believe, be carried on in the replanning of existing

zoos or the setting out of new ones. London has already
done much in this direction; the ungulates on the Cotton
Terrace were among the first to enjoy far greater freedom than they had been used to. Basle will stay longest
in my memory. I was tremendously impressed by what
must be the finest collection of elephants anywhere in
the world. African and Indian varieties do not usually
mix well together, but here there was not the slightest
sign of trouble. Bath time, when some seven or eight
elephants took their daily ducking, was a sight I would
not have thought possible. First, the keepers enter the
line of stalls from the back and hose down the elephants;
then each animal steps forward into the bath in front
of its den and rolls over in the water. At the same time a
small army of boys and girls clamber all over the partly
submerged giants and scrub away with long-handled
brooms at the parts showing above the water. When one
side is clean, the order is given to 'turn over', and the
operation repeated. I understood that the cleaning
squad were all volunteers for the day and there was
always a long waiting list of youngsters keen to help out.
You can imagine the amount of water that was being
splashed about, sometimes swamping visitors, and the
whole building rang with the laughter of people enjoying a most hilarious spectacle. During the afternoon
the same elephants plodded happily around a circular
track carrying children on their backs and then at the
end of the day they put on a special performance for
us in a small circus ring. The affection the animals had
for their trainer proved that his control over them had
been achieved by kindness alone. In most zoos where

elephants are kept the matter of suitable exercise is a problem. In Basle the riding stints provide enough action to keep away boredom during the summer months, and in the winter the animals are taken out on long walks through the forest and the town.

The Continental zoos which we saw had better presentation, mainly because good use had been made of the available space; but London had by far the greater variety in its exhibits.

JOS ZOO, NIGERIA

Two or three weeks before I completed my service I was asked if I would be prepared to go out to Nigeria for three months. I was thrilled at the prospect. Like so many animal lovers, I had often expressed a desire to visit Africa and see wild life 'at home'. Apparently the little zoo at Jos on the plateau in northern Nigeria was still experiencing teething troubles, despite being in existence for some ten years, and had appealed to London Zoo for help.

On 16 February 1969 when I left London Airport, the temperature was below freezing point and after a flight of some eight hours with a refuelling stop at Rome, I landed at Kano in a sweltering heat, though it was still only 7 o'clock in the morning. I had given up hope of ever seeing Africa, now I was here, still marvelling at the sight which greeted me when I opened my eyes after a cat-nap on the plane, looked out and saw dawn breaking over the desert. How best to describe such fantastic beauty is well beyond me, I only know that I sat transfixed until we began our descent and I am sure there could have been no better way of introduction. A small aircraft took me on to Jos and soon after eight o'clock I was being shown around the zoo by the honorary secretary, Geoffrey Watson. My first impression was not a happy one; obviously there was much to do to improve the standard and, with the very limited labour force, the task looked rather formidable. The 'Zukepas' numbered only half a dozen; about the same number of men made up the works or maintenance department; apart from a manager and a technician these were the total staff. With the exception of the secretary, all were Nigerian and very little English was spoken. At the first opportunity I called a meeting which was attended by all the workers and with the help of the technician, who acted as interpreter, I had a frank discussion about what had to be done, and how I intended to do it.

Having overcome their initial suspicions, I got them to accept the fact that I had not come to make trouble for them, merely to help and advise. My theme was that, were it not for the animals, they themselves would not be needed, and neglect of their duties would have disastrous results on them and their families. I made a practice of meeting with them every Saturday evening; although the get-togethers were labelled 'educational' classes, many were the human problems I was called upon to judge. In this way I was able to win both respect and confidence from a group of people almost child-like in their simplicity of mind, and the understanding between us got better all the time. The keepers

lacked nothing in courage—indeed the risks they ran
could be frightening—but they were extremely casual
towards the animals in their care. Perhaps for too long
anything from the bush had only been thought of in
terms of food or pelt value, and my first obligation was
to promote some completely new train of thought in
their minds.

Luckily I had taken with me many photographs
which acted as visual proof of what could be accom-
plished with patience and kindness; these certainly
sparked off a new interest and we began to operate on
the same wavelength. For the first time, these men had
found someone willing and eager to spell things out for
them and, though the lessons were elementary in the
extreme, the delight expressed by their faces as they
were able to supply the answers to simple questions
showed we were on the right track. When they began to
learn what is meant by a marsupial; the difference in
markings between the leopard and the cheetah; the fact
that they themselves were mammals like the animals
in the enclosures; then it was a case of one at a time as
they loudly competed against each other in 'school'.
Without a doubt, the most enjoyable lesson as far as
they were concerned was when I organised an escaped
animal drill. Acting the role of a hyena on the loose, I
allowed myself to be chased all round the zoo before
being finally cornered and recaptured. The buttons on
the uniforms almost burst with pride and the fact that
visitors were witness to the keepers' cleverness meant
added satisfaction. I am certain they will never forget
the day when 'Sir' showed them how it is done and how

nice it was to play a game at the same time. As for
'Sir', he needed a couple of hours to recuperate
after chasing around in the heat, but it was time well
spent.

Hygiene was the next most important matter to be
put right and the fact that utensils used for cleaning
must not in any circumstances be used for carrying
food was but one of the many corrections. As the weeks
went by, a distinct improvement in the bearing of the
uniformed staff became noticeable and, because they
were becoming more able to converse with and answer
questions put by visitors, their own interpretation of
what it means to be a keeper got a great deal nearer to
the required standard.

On Easter Monday morning I was making my daily
inspection when I was approached by the lady curator
of the nearby museum. She told me that a hyena had
been sighted a mile or so away and she would rather
like me to do something about it. I replied that the zoo
already had three and I very much doubted whether
there was any danger to human life, but to pacify her
I agreed to go along. The staff was overjoyed at the
prospect of the real thing so soon after they had proved
themselves in practice, but I made them contain themselves until I had taken a closer look at the situation. I
was driven away in a car carrying a police superinten-
dent, a constable armed with a rifle, and two ladies from
the museum as extra passengers, and had to promise to
send back for my enthusiastic staff should I need any
extra help. Arriving at the place where the animal had
been sighted, I looked up to the entrance to a cave high

among the rocks and began to climb. The thought going through my mind was how to get a trapping box in position if the situation demanded. A shout from below caused me to look up just in time to see a brown shape rush out of the cave and disappear over the summit, but not before I had been able to identify it as a dog. A flood of relief went through me, for if a dog was around it was certain there was no hyena in the vicinity. Soon afterwards whimpering puppy cries greeted me as I reached the cave, where four wriggling little shapes were registering protest at the sudden departure of their mother. A poor under-fed bedraggled bitch, seeking a quiet place to give birth to her puppies, was the cause of all the excitement. She had been briefly sighted by a native policeman as he cycled along the nearby track and imagination had done the rest.

The evenings in Nigeria are short; at 6.30 it was full daylight, by 7.30 there was complete darkness, but to me that last hour was one of rare beauty. Leaving the zoo about 6 o'clock I would walk a short distance to the big rambling house which had been put at my disposal, have a cooler under the shower and sit out on the porch. I would watch the comings and goings of scarlet weavers and other gloriously coloured small birds; the busy search for food by dozens of curious little chameleon-like lizards, and vultures wheeling high above as they waited to descend to roost. From the hills came the chanting of the tribesmen and suddenly I would begin to feel like an intruder and awfully lonely. This loneliness fortunately was soon eliminated as I began to

F

meet and make friends with some of the many expatri-
ates serving out their careers in Jos. 'Come to the house
for a meal' became almost a daily invitation, and I was
given a warm welcome at the clubs. The Europeans
were all extremely fond of animals and their assistance
in rearing young stock, tending the sick, even dipping
into their own pockets to buy exhibits for the zoo was
of immense help for a little organisation with a limited
income. In one home you would see a baby chimpanzee
being bottle-fed with loving care; at another you would
find a young caracal lynx being hand-reared until such
time as it would fend for itself when returned to the
zoo. Send out an SOS for help and there was always
someone ready to answer the call; without these people
Jos Zoo would be in dire straits.

It was little short of a miracle to discover that the
litter brother of Rabiu, the cheetah, was here at Jos. In
less than a week Mailafia, meaning 'the Happy One',
was enjoying his first walk outside his enclosure as I
quickly trained him to a collar and chain. It was heart-
breaking to find such a delightfully well-dispositioned
animal with ears half eaten away by the thousands of
flies which are such a curse in Nigeria. Mailafia received
intensive treatment because he could be handled so
easily, but nothing could be done to replace the lost
pieces. He was put on a powdered milk diet for the first
time, enjoyed a walk and a grooming every morning,
and was allowed an occasional visitor. Now perhaps he
felt more like living up to his name. The flies also
affected the three lions, although treatment here would
have been more complicated; with the harm already

done, all I could do was to order a heap of bracken to be put into the enclosure so that if the torment became too much they could push their heads into it to brush off the flies.

I found another real treasure in Candy, the leopardess, and very soon we were playing games of hide and seek. As I came towards her cage, Candy would crouch down behind the stonework in the front section of her den and all I could see would be the tips of her ears flicking with excitement. When I was about twenty yards away she would rush to the back of the cage and hide behind a big rock which served as a shelf for her to lie on. Finding the cage apparently empty, I would go to the one spot where I could reach over to pet her through the wire netting and softly call to her. She would remain out of sight until I said something like, 'OK, I'll go and leave you'; then she would jump to roll over on her back, purring her pleasure, and finally pressing hard against the netting so that I could stroke her neck and fondle her ears. Poor Candy had a permanent limp. Two young native boys had bound her to a cross pole slung between their shoulders as they carried her around looking for a buyer, and it was a merciful blessing that she was rescued by one of the Europeans. He told me it took many weeks of careful nursing before Candy could walk again. Even today she bears the marks where the thongs cut into the flesh of her right foreleg.

As the zoo began to show improvement, with the staff taking a much keener interest in their charges, I accepted an invitation to visit Colonel 'Bill' Barlow, vice-president of the Jos Zoological Society, and his charming wife, Dorothy, at their home some thirty miles out of town. On arrival there I found a little menagerie of small West African mammals and birds, and a splendid Alsatian bitch, Rani, and her two pups. During the evening an 8ft-long python was produced and handled with the sureness of people who could never harm any living thing and had only love for the creatures round them. Talk turned to the game reserve at Yankari, up in the Bauchie State, and Bill offered to take me there as soon as he could spare the time from his mining business. This was the one thing I would have chosen had someone invited me to make a wish. The prospect of my dream coming true was enough to keep me awake half the night as I waited out the next two weeks.

At the zoo, the lioness became pregnant; I ordered extra rations for her and marked the calendar to show when the cubs were expected. Judy Block, an American hoping to make a career as a zoologist who had been holding the fort prior to my arrival, returned from a trip to the Lake Chad area, bringing with her a young female Situtunga. One of the larger-type bucks, this animal is most happy living in swamp conditions; so a pond was built in her enclosure, with earth, bracken and the like used to create natural conditions. Just to add variety, a young camel also arrived as a gift. As Geoffrey Watson had on more than one occasion taken charge of a camel train in his younger days, I was happy to let him supervise its needs.

YANKARI GAME RESERVE

Eventually Bill and I set off on our trip and drove the 200 miles to Yankari. Almost as soon as we had passed the entrance gate, he stopped the car and we walked amongst the many baboons who make their home at Wicky Wells, so named because of the many deep well-like holes dotted around. These make ideal homes for the baboons who were not unduly worried by our presence, but I noticed the old male sentinel standing guard ready to give the 'Take off to the trees' order at the first sign of interference. We motored on to the camp site and then made our way down to the fabulous Wicky Springs, where the water entering the pool from under the high rock face remains at a temperature of about 80° all the year round, day and night. It was sheer bliss to float in the pool and let the running water wash away the grime of the long journey.

Next morning at 6.30 we climbed aboard the truck which was to take us on a conducted tour of the reserve. I quickly got on good terms with our native guide, although my part of the conversation consisted of pidgin English and hand signs. On our first run we saw hundreds of wart hogs, those quaint pig-like animals which live in family groups and, when disturbed, set off at a fast run, their little legs going like clockwork and their tails standing bolt upright. They always travel in single file, Dad leading, and Mum and the offspring sprinting along, seemingly in order of seniority; the last thing you see as they disappear into the bush is a backside belonging to the baby. Baboons and various types of monkey jabbered at us as we slowly drove under their tree-top homes, and herds of gazelles sped away at our approach. Some of the large ungulates, like the hartebeest, were not so shy and remained close enough for other members of our party to get some good shots—with a camera. Towards the end of the run we were very fortunate in seeing the rare secretary bird, so named because its head feathers give the impression of a quill pen behind the ear, and the beautiful white sacred ibis.

We were out early again next day. Our travelling companions were four Sisters of the Order of St David, and from the moment we set off I rather sensed that one of them was paying close attention to me from the opposite seat; each time I looked in her direction, she shyly dropped her eyes. 'Well, if we are to be in each other's company for the next two hours we may as well introduce ourselves,' said Bill. 'This is Mr Alldis. He has come from the London Zoo to help us at Jos, and my name is Barlow.' As he spoke, a complete change of expression came over the face of the young sister and she said, 'Ah, that is where I have seen you, I was there last September with a party from Portsmouth and I remember you being in the cheetah's cage when we passed.' Although we saw plenty of wild life, there was still no sign of elephant. This had been the sisters' last opportunity of seeing any as they were leaving the camp that day.

A few hours later, the time-worn phrase 'It's a small world' was once more repeated. Bill and I had joined a gathering down at the pool, when a young married couple informed us that they lived in south-west London and one of the husband's closest friends was a young man who, as a boy, used to spend hours in the garden driving an imaginary railway engine and wearing a discarded London Zoo keeper's cap provided by me. That same evening we made our final run, for we had to return to Jos the next day. We were joined by Judy Block, who had come up to Yankari to do an elephant survey, although she admitted that all she had seen so far were the tracks of small herds. Selecting an entirely new area for exploration, we set off more in hope than expectation.

For about an hour we drove along and my notebook recorded the fact that we had seen twenty-two varieties of mammals and birds, which must have made the trip worthwhile; but still we had not sighted any elephants and had a feeling of a slight let-down. As dusk began to fall, we decided to go the shortest way back to camp and turned on to a little used track. Suddenly the truck stopped and our guide motioned us to silence as he pointed to a thick bush on our left and there, not more than a hundred yards away but almost invisible, stood a lone male elephant. As the big shape began to move into a clearing, the animal walked parallel to our path until he was well clear of the truck and then crossed the trail to disappear from view. So we set off again and Judy ticked a single entry on her information form. When the truck halted again and the guide, with the usual warning gestures, pointed across the wide clearing, I sensed rather than saw the waving of branches of trees, as though a strong wind was blowing high on the trail leading to the clearing. In a moment or so came the sound of those branches being snapped off as down the trail came elephants of all sizes, males and females, from the big bull down to the babies frolicking along behind their mothers. While they gathered at the meeting point, I told Judy their approximate ages and sex and she scribbled away madly in her anxiety to record all the information she could. As we waited there in the gathering darkness, it seemed as though the herd decided to put on a special show as a reward for our patience, for having posted a look-out about half-way between the truck and themselves they began the serious business of their ablutions. Whilst some of them rubbed against the trees to relieve itchy spots, others gathered up damp, sandy soil with their trunks and sprayed it over their backs and between their front legs. When everything had been done to their satisfaction they re-formed into single file and slowly made off to the bedding ground, the look-out being last to rejoin the group. By the time we got back to camp it was completely dark and the first people we met were the sisters just about to make their departure. We described our good fortune and expressed our sincere regret that they had not been with us. Bless their hearts, they were not a bit envious and were only happy that we ourselves had had such a successful run. That night the heat was so intense that everyone slept with the chalet windows or doors open and the baboons made the most of the opportunity to come inside and look for foodstuffs and anything bright, such as jewellery or cigarette lighters, that careless visitors may have left within reach, for such things have a distinct fascination for them.

The following morning we started the long drive back to Jos, but on the way Bill stopped the car at the emir's palace and, being well known to the ruler, was granted an audience in his private room. I greatly appreciated the honour of being present, and with Bill acting as interpreter exchanged pleasantries with the emir, who, when it was time to go, walked arm-in-arm with me to the courtyard and held a huge umbrella over me in the torrential rainstorm which had suddenly started and stood bareheaded to wave good-bye as we drove away. Bill informed me that such treatment was usually reserved for the all powerful ones, so I rather pride myself that I must have created a good impression.

The remaining few weeks at Jos Zoo passed very quickly: there were still many things to be done, not the least important being the preparation of my final report to the council and recommendations for future policy. As a token of thanks for my efforts I was presented with the official tie and made an honorary life member. On 8 May, just short of three months since I had arrived, I was driven out to the airport, where many of my new-found friends were waiting to bid me farewell and a safe journey home.

Conclusion

In my forty-one years at the London Zoo many changes have taken place. For instance, up to 1939 the area formerly known as the Elephant Walk was the busiest, noisiest and most certainly the happiest spot in the gardens. Long seats placed end to end stretched for some eighty yards on either side of it and, in between, the elephants slowly made their way up and down, with their cargoes of happy children. The time the journey took depended largely on the amount of buns, apples, bananas or other choice tit-bits in the possession of people on the sidelines. If these were not offered quickly enough an elephant would pick up a hat, a handbag or anything else within reach of its trunk, make a pretence of transferring the article to its mouth and finally hand it up to the keeper riding on its neck. It was when the elephantine mouth opened wide as if to make a meal of the plunder that the roars of laughter from the crowd broke out and very often the owner of the article laughed as loudly as anybody. During the war the elephants were evacuated to the country zoo at Whipsnade where rides did continue for a time with old Dixie, an Indian female. But they were never restarted in London; somehow the present-day rides on camels, llamas and ponies seem very tame by comparision. The famous Walk has been used as building space to house gibbons and macaws.

I feel that the Zoo is not quite the place it used to be for the family man. At one time the entrance fee was a shilling and half-price for a child under fourteen, so the whole family could do themselves proud on ten shillings; today that would just about gain admittance for Dad alone and leave enough for a pamphlet guide! Even the feeding of animals by the public is no longer allowed; this ban was introduced in 1968 so that some measure of control could be exercised over diets. Anything that benefits animals has my wholehearted approval, but why it was thought necessary to include all the inmates is something that is open to argument. In the old days, especially at the week-ends, something was happening all day long at the Zoo to provide that little extra in the way of pleasure and entertainment, something that people could go home and tell their neighbours about. The polar bears diving into the pool at feeding time, in addition to the public show at 3pm, was a spectacle to be enjoyed a dozen times a day. The penguin shows; feeding the sea-lions, with the high dive of the old 'Bull' as the star turn; the chimpanzees taken from their cages to accept the fruit offerings from their admirers; the pygmy hippos and their not so little relations opening those cavernous jaws to take in whole cabbages—all these and many more could be witnessed as the visitor walked around, in addition to the Chimps' Tea Party and public feeds. An even more important factor was that a large number of animals could look forward to a repeat performance in the near future and thus have 'something to live for'. Today, the official feeding times and the Chimps' Tea Party are the sole survivors, and if you miss these there is no chance of a repeat.

The Zoo's collection is probably second to none, but now it has to be admired at a more respectful distance, and maybe it is the absence of some of the previous intimacies that is partly the cause of a falling off at the turnstiles. People the world over will pay to see animals. Whether or not the safari parks will eventually put the zoos out of business is anybody's guess, but the competition is real and it is up to the zoo authorities to offer more value for money.

Working in what to me were ideal conditions, knowledge came mostly through close and careful study of my charges. My devotion to them and their affection for me were emotions much more freely expressed because of the opportunities that existed then. I have the feeling that the old-time keeper is a dying race: too many youngsters today would much rather be given a verbal explanation of an everyday problem than find out the answer for themselves. Perhaps there is less encouragement nowadays for keepers to form attachments with their charges, and greater consideration given to lectures and courses; but generally speaking the practical side lags behind, in my opinion.

Many times I have enjoyed a joke with my charges; the closer the contact between you, the more often you could share a confidence that would be completely lost to anyone else. I know many of my readers have felt a grievous loss at the passing of their dog, cat, bird, or any other pet they had grown to love. Magnify this ten times and you get an idea of how it feels when a zoo keeper says a final good-bye to an old friend. Every good dog has a good master; one makes the other, but no one ever masters the proud, aloof dignity of a captive animal. When it gives you its confidence and affection, it gives you plenty. One thing it will never give is its own self respect, and he would be a foolish man who expected it. Most dogs will give blind obedience, even to the extent of being made to look foolish, but no lion, tiger, leopard, cheetah or other such specimen should ever be made an object of ridicule. I do not refer to some circus animals or to the primates, who will perform some really hilarious turns with apparent enjoyment in return for a reward. Rightly or wrongly, however, I feel at least partly qualified to give a viewpoint on animals in the zoo. The caged animal relies on his keeper for its all, and if, in the giving and taking, friendship is formed, this becomes a bond, a valuable two-way relationship. A sensible person can win the affection of his dog and enjoy its comradeship with little or no risk of injury. If he upsets his pet it will keep its distance and, by so doing, show its feelings, but without lasting effect. With a captive animal there is a marked difference. There comes a time when it is necessary to enter its cage, when man and beast have to trust one another. If you have given the animal cause to dislike you, he will not keep his distance. You are in his domain and he will make the most of his opportunity by attacking. When you are able to walk into a cage or den without any thoughts of being attacked, when you are received as a friend and treated as such, this is the time that pays for all the long hours spent in patiently breaking through the natural reserve, and slowly day by day driving out fear and overcoming mistrust.

For the animal, the value of the relationship is that its life is so much more settled; it feels secure knowing that its friend is there to protect it. Oh yes, believe me, they come to rely on protection; even the mesh wire, which is a safety measure for the public, gives a great deal of comfort to the one on the inside. Next time you visit a zoo, take particular notice of the animals that spend most of their waking hours as far away as possible from the visitors; these are the shy, nervous types. Those that are always to the forefront are the ones that have found that one side of the barrier is theirs alone. Should anyone cross the safety barrier and lay a hand on the actual netting, each type will react, though in a different way. The shy ones will endeavour to get even farther away, and the not so shy will attack and do all they can to drive away the trespasser. In an instant their whole character changes and they remain on edge long after the offender has been removed. If people sometimes stopped to consider the keeper, who may have to enter the cage of an animal shortly after it has been upset, then perhaps they would be more careful to obey the regulations.

I would be the first to admit that my own career in the service of the Zoological Society of London was blessed with remarkable good fortune. The wind of change blows in many directions and the opportunities that existed in my day may no longer be there for the taking, but in all sincerity I do assure young keepers that theirs is a life to be envied, a profession to be proud of and, if they do their job to the best of their ability, they will find, as I did, that the animals in their charge are also their friends.

Many people ask, 'Don't you miss it all?' Well, of course, I do. I miss the bustle and the cheery chatter of the holiday crowds. I miss the chance to meet famous people. Certainly I will never again be able to travel to the extent I did in the service of the Zoo. I miss the friendship of many animal lovers, who made my job so much easier and the lives of my charges so much happier. But, above all, I miss my animals; they were some of my best friends, after all.